Also by Sydney Foster

Keto Diet Coach

Ketogenic Diet Guide for Beginners: Easy Weight Loss with Plans and Recipes (Keto Cookbook, Complete Lifestyle Plan)

Instant Pot for Two Cookbook: Easy and Delicious Recipes (Slow Cooker for 2, Healthy Dishes)

Ketogenic Instant Pot Cookbook: Easy, Delicious Recipes for Weight Loss (Pressure Cooker Meals, Quick Healthy Eating, Meal Plan)

Ketogenic Diet Recipes in 20 Minutes or Less:: Beginner's Weight Loss Keto Cookbook Guide (Ketogenic Cookbook, Complete Lifestyle Plan)

Standalone

Instant Pot for Two Cookbook for Beginners: A Mother's Guide

Table of Contents

Instant Pot Cookbook for Two Cookbook for Beginners

A Mother's Guide

Sydney Foster © 2019

Introduction

The Instant pot is the future of the kitchen, especially if you're a single parent. Most people think that instant pot can only be used when cooking for a large family, but this simply isn't true. Instant pots are a useful kitchen tool that allows you to cook delicious dishes in no time at all. It helps to replace pots, stoves, pans and ovens, so cooking becomes a lot easier and a lot more fun.

About the Instant Pot

If you've purchased an instant pot, you probably can't wait to use it, but you should familiarize yourself with the different pressure release methods to make sure that you use it safely. There are two ways that you can relieve pressure with your instant pot. There is the quick release and the natural pressure release. The quick release is where you open your valve manually so that the steam releases quickly. The float valve will sink when all the pressure is released which will allow the lid to unlock. The lid will not open until the float valve drops because it is a safety mechanism.

The natural pressure release is where you allow the pressure to decrease without opening the valve. After the cooking time is up, the instant pot will switch from cooking to keep warm. At this time the pressure will naturally drop. The pressure is naturally dropping during this time, and the time will depend on just how much liquid is in your pot. It can take as little as ten minutes to a half an hour. Always go with what the recipe says, but if you're trying new recipes, you'll want a quick release for anything that will get soggy if overcooked. A natural pressure release is better for things that can simmer such as meats, soups and stews.

The Buttons

There are manual settings that you can use with your instant pot but there is also preselected cooking routines that you can access with a push of a button. In some instant pots there is even a timer that will delay the start time for up to twenty-four hours. Here are a few common buttons.

- **Manual:** You use this setting if you want to adjust the pressure and cooking time. Most recipes use the manual setting.
- **Sauté:** This allows you to adjust from frying to simmer. You use it to heat foods and thicken sauces.
- **Slow Cook:** You use this to use your instant pot as you would a slow cooker. To use tis setting turn the pressure release to the venting position.
- **Keep Warm/Cancel:** This will cancel your setting while still keeping your food warm.
- **Soup:** You'll see this for soups, which cooks for forty minutes at high pressure. You can still adjust the time manually.
- **Meat/Stew:** This cooks at high pressure for thirty-five minutes. You can adjust the cooking time manually.
- **Bean/Chili:** This cooks at high pressure for a half hour. You can adjust the cooking time manually.
- **Rice:** This prepares rice, and you cannot adjust the cooking time manually.
- **Poultry:** this cooks chicken or other poultry for fifteen minutes at high pressure. You can adjust the cooking time manually.
- **Porridge:** This cooks oatmeal and porridge at high pressure for twenty minutes. You can adjust the cooking time manually.
- **Multigrain:** This cooks at high pressure for forty minutes, but the cooking time can be adjusted manually.
- **Steam:** You use this to steam foods, including vegetables, using a steamer basket. It cooks at high pressure for ten minutes.

A Nutrition Breakdown

...take a simple look a nutrition. This chapter is meant to serve as a guideline, but ...a grain of salt. Do what you can to create healthy meals, made easy with the ...he pleasures of life with comfort foods and desserts. Just always choose wisely. ...n.

Quality of Calories

You already know what calories are, and there's no reason to count them if you're maintaining a healthy weight. Instead, you know the quality of calories that you're taking in. not all calories are equal to each other after all. Your body will digest different nutrients differently. Some will help with building muscles, others will help with fueling organs, some will be stored as fat, and so on.

- **Protein:** Your muscles are broken down when you exercise, and they need protein to help rebuild themselves. Protein should be in every meal. You can get protein from quinoa, legumes, nuts, fish, pork, beef, eggs, chicken and a lot of dairy products.
- **Carbohydrates:** Also known as carbs, these are converted to sugar. This is then used as an energy source for your body. You can get quality carbs from vegetables and fruit. Grains aren't considered quality carbs, and you'll want to avoid processed carbs whenever possible.
- **Fat:** This is a misunderstood macro-nutrient. Fat should be a large portion of your calories. Good fats include walnuts, almonds, avocados, and olive oil. These are healthy fats also known as polyunsaturated or monounsaturated fats. It's saturated fat that you need to be weary of. Fatty cuts of meat, full fat milk and even coconut milk can have bad fats, but that doesn't mean they need to be avoided entirely either.

Fat Doesn't Make You Fat

The first thing you need to realize is that fat doesn't make you fat. Which is why fat free or low fat food isn't necessarily healthy. It's refined carbs, processed carbs and simple sugars that are making people fat. While you can still indulge in these as well, you need to make sure that you do it in moderation and have adequate exercise in yours and your child's daily routine to counterbalance it. Just make an educated choice.

Avoid Over Eating

Over eating can be difficult on the body. While it' okay t over indulge sometimes, you should leave these days few and far between. Your body can only burn away so many calories a day, and those excess calories are stored as fat. That's why it's important to try to eat healthy, especially if you're going to splurge later in the day. remember that your body will burn a small amount of calories even if you live an inactive lifestyle, but it won't usually burn nearly enough to keep you from storing some fat if you aren't exercising.

The Dangers of Leftovers

You'll notice that all of the recipes in this book are designed to only serve two people once. This way you don't have any leftovers. Leftovers can be dangerous because you often won't use them for the next day. Instead, it tempts you towards that second helping that won't help you to stay healthy and maintain a proper weight. It's even more tempting when the food is great or something that you shouldn't be eating in the first place. Which is why this book does not allow for left overs. Cooking a fresh meal each and every day is made simpler with the instant pot because you won't be slaving away in the kitchen for hours. So ditch the left overs and eat healthy portions only once. This way you won't get tired of eating the same food all of the time either!

Try to Skip Snacks & Desserts

While it's okay to have snacks, appetizers and desserts occasionally. You should try to at least make it where you're eating these every other day. This is another great way to make sure that you aren't getting too many calories in a single day. Of course, snacks, appetizers and desserts often are a host of simple sugars, simple carbs, and empty calories, so if you can save them for only once or twice a week, that's even better. Still, everyone likes to indulge sometimes, which is why they've been included in this recipe book.

Breakfast Recipes

Here are some breakfast recipes to get you started! You'll find a lot of them are under a half hour for those much needed ready to go breakfasts for any busy mother.

Cherry Apple Risotto

Serves: 2

Time: 25 Minutes

Ingredients:

- 1 Apple, Peeled, Cored & Diced
- ¾ Cup Risotto Rice
- 1 ½ Cups Milk
- ¼ Cup Brown Sugar
- ½ Cup Apple Juice
- ¾ Teaspoon Cinnamon
- ¼ Cup Cherries, Dried
- 1 Tablespoon Butter

Directions:

1. Press sauté, and then add in your butter. Cook for four minutes so that it turns opaque.
2. Mix in your spices, brown sugar, apples, and stir well. Pouring your milk and juice, stirring well.
3. Cook on high pressure, and then use a quick release.
4. Add in your dried cherries, stirring well.
5. Serve with a splash of milk and sprinkled with almonds and brown sugar.

Pistachio Quinoa

Serves: 2

Time: 1 Hour 15 Minutes

Ingredients:

- ¾ Cup White Quinoa
- 1/8 Cup Raisins
- ½ Cup Apple Juice
- ½ Cup Yogurt, Plain
- ½ Tablespoon Honey, Raw
- ¾ Cup Water
- 1 Small Cinnamon Stick
- 3 Tablespoons Blueberries
- 1/8 Cup Pistachios, Chopped

Directions:

1. Rinse your quinoa before straining it through a fine mesh.
2. Add your water, quinoa, and cinnamon into your instant pot, and then cook on high pressure for a minute. Allow for a natural pressure release.
3. Spoon your quinoa into a bowl, removing your cinnamon.
4. Add in your remaining ingredients except for your yogurt, and allow it to cool in the fridge for an hour.
5. Add in your yogurt before serving, stirring well. Top with pistachios and serve chilled.

Cheesy Grits

Serves: 2

Time: 25 Minutes

Ingredients

- 1 Cup Water
- 2 Cups Old Fashion Grits
- 2 Tablespoons Butter
- 2 Cups Milk
- ½ Cup Cheddar Cheese, Shredded
- Sea Salt & Black Pepper to Taste

Directions:

1. Mix all of your ingredients together, and then cook on low pressure.
2. Use a natural pressure release for ten minutes before using a quick release.
3. Sprinkle with cheese, whisking before serving.

Banana Porridge

Serves: 20 Minutes
Time: 15 Minutes
Ingredients:

- ½ Cup Macadamia Nuts, Ground
- ½ Cup Green Apple, Grated
- ½ Cup Berries, Fresh & Mixed
- ½ Teaspoon Cinnamon
- ½ Teaspoon Ground Clove
- 2 Tablespoons Chia Seeds
- 1 Cup Bananas, Ripe
- 1 ¼ Cups Coconut Milk

Directions:

1. Add all of your ingredients except for your berries into your instant pot.
2. Cook on high pressure for six minutes.
3. Use a quick release, and top with berries before serving.

Creamy Eggs

Serves: 2

Time: 15 Minutes

Ingredients:

- 2 Eggs
- ½ Tablespoons Chives, Fresh & Minced
- 2 Tablespoons Cream
- Sea Salt & Black Pepper to Taste

Directions:

1. Start by greasing two ramekins, and then put a tablespoon of cream into each one.
2. Crack an egg into each one before sprinkling them with chives.
3. Add a cup of water into the bottom of your instant pot before placing your trivet in it.
4. Put your ramekins in your trivet, and then cook on high pressure for two minutes.
5. Use a quick release, and season with salt and pepper before serving.

Eggs in a Cup

Serves: 2

Time: 20 Minutes

Ingredients:

- 2 Eggs
- 2 Bell Peppers
- 1 Tablespoon Mozzarella Cheese, Grated Fresh
- 2 Bread Slices, Toasted
- Sea Salt & Black Pepper to Taste

Directions:

1. Cut the ends off of your bell peppers to form 1 ½ inch high cups, and then take out the seeds.
2. Crack an egg into each, and cover them with foil.
3. Place one and a half cups of water into your instant pot before adding your steamer basket.
4. Put the bell peppers on top of your steamer basket, cooking on low pressure for four minutes.
5. Use a quick release, and then sprinkle your cheese over it. Sprinkle with salt and pepper and serve with bread.

Espresso Oatmeal

Serves: 2

Time: 20 Minutes

Ingredients:

- 1 Teaspoon Vanilla Extract
- ½ Cup Milk
- ½ Teaspoon Espresso Powder
- 1 Tablespoon White Sugar
- ½ Cup Steel Cut oats
- 1 ¼ Cups Water
- Pinch Salt
- Grated Chocolate for Serving
- Whipped Cream for Serving

Directions:

1. Mix your water, oats, sugar, milk, and salt and espresso powder together in your instant pot. Stir, and cover. Cook on high pressure for ten minutes. Use a quick release.
2. Add in your vanilla extract, stirring again. Cover, and allow it to sit for five minutes before serving with chocolate and whipped cream.

Healthy Rice Pudding

Serves: 2

Time: 30 Minutes

Ingredients:

- 1 Cup Water
- 1 Cup Basmati Rice
- 1 Cup Milk
- 2 Tablespoons Maple Syrup
- 4 Tablespoons Heavy Cream
- ½ Teaspoon Vanilla Extract, Pure
- Pinch Salt

Directions:

1. In your instant pot mix your water, rice, milk, and maple syrup together. Stir until well combined.
2. Cover, cooking on high pressure for twenty minutes. Use a quick release.
3. Add in your vanilla extract and cream, stirring well.
4. Serve warm.

Ham Casserole

Serves: 2
Time: 35 Minutes

Ingredients:

- 4 Red Potatoes, Cubed
- 1 Cup Cheddar Cheese, Shredded
- 1 Cup Ham, Chopped
- ½ Yellow Onion, Chopped
- 6 Eggs
- 1 Cup Milk
- 2 Cups Water
- Sea Salt & Black Pepper to Taste

Directions:

1. Start by mixing your salt, eggs, and milk together. Add in your potatoes, ham, pepper, onion, and cheese before whisking well.
2. Spray down your pan with cooking oil, and put the water into your instant pot, adding in a steamer basket. Add the pan with your egg mix on top of the steamer basket, and cook for twenty-five minutes. Use a quick release.
3. Leave you casserole to cool, and slice to serve.

Strawberry Quinoa Bowl

Serves: 2

Time: 12 Minutes

Ingredients:

- 1 Tablespoon Honey, Raw
- 1 ½ Cups Water
- ½ Teaspoon Vanilla Extract, Pure
- 1 Cup Quinoa
- Pinch Pumpkin Pie Spice
- 1 Cup Strawberries, Sliced
- ½ Cup Vanilla Yogurt

Directions:

1. Put your quinoa, water, honey, pumpkin pie spice, vanilla, strawberries and yogurt into your instant pot. Stir well.
2. Cook on high pressure for a minute. Allow for a natural pressure release for ten minutes before using a quick release for the remaining pressure.
3. Set it to the side of ten minutes, and fluff with a fork before serving.

Simple Egg Bake

Serves: 2

Time: 30 Minutes

Ingredients:

- 3 Bacon Slices, Chopped
- 1 Cup Hash Browns
- 2 Tablespoons Milk
- ¼ Cup Cheddar Cheese, Shredded
- 3 Eggs
- 1 Small Red Bell Pepper, Chopped
- 1 ½ Cups Water
- 2 Mushrooms, Chopped
- Sea Salt & Black Pepper to Taste

Directions:

1. Press sauté on the instant pot, adding in your bacon. Cook for a couple of minutes before adding in your mushrooms and bell pepper
2. Allow the mixture to cook for three more minutes before adding in your hash browns.
3. Cook for two minutes before transferring everything to a bowl. Clean out your instant pot.
4. Add in your milk, salt, pepper, eggs and cheese into the bowl along with your vegetables and ham. Whisk well, and transfer into a greased dish.
5. Add your water to your instant pot, and then put in your steamer basket. Put the dish inside, covering and cooking for ten minutes on high pressure. Use a quick release.
6. Allow it to cool before serving.

Breakfast Quiche

Serves: 2

Time: 40 Minutes

Ingredients:

- 3 Eggs
- ¼ Cup Milk
- 1 Cup Water
- ½ Cup Cheddar Cheese, Shredded
- 1 Tablespoon Chives, Chopped
- Sea Salt & Black Pepper to taste

Directions:

1. Mix your eggs, salt, pepper, milk and chives together in a bowl, mixing well.
2. Get out a cake pan and wrap it with foil, creasing it with cooking spray. Put your cheese in the pan before pouring your egg mixture over it. Make sure it's spread out evenly.
3. Add the water to your instant pot before placing the steamer basket inside.
4. Put the cake pan on the steamer basket, cooking on high pressure for thirty minutes before using a quick release.
5. Serve warm.

Simple French Toast

Serves: 2

Time: 35 Minutes

Ingredients:

- 1 Tablespoon Cream Cheese
- 2 Eggs
- 2 Bananas, Sliced
- 1 Tablespoon Brown Sugar
- 3 French Bread Slices, Cubed
- ¼ Cup Milk
- ½ Tablespoon White Sugar
- ½ Teaspoon Vanilla Extract, Pure
- Pinch of Cinnamon
- 1 Tablespoon Butter
- 2 Tablespoons Pecans, Chopped
- ¾ Cup Water

Directions:

1. Grease a cooking dish, and then add your bread cubes on the bottom.
2. Layer your banana slices, sprinkling with brown sugar.
3. Add in your melted cream cheese, spreading it out in an even layer.
4. Add the rest of your bread cubes, and then add more banana slices butter, and then sprinkle in half of your pecans.
5. Get out a bowl, mixing your white sugar, cinnamon, vanilla and milk together until well combined.
6. Pour this over your pan, and add water into your instant pot.
7. Place a trivet into your instant pot, putting your pan on top. Cover, cooking on high for twenty-five minutes. Use a quick release.
8. Sprinkle with the rest of the pecans before serving.

Burrito Casserole

Serves: 2

Time: 25 Minutes

Ingredients:

- 2 Eggs
- Sea Salt & Black Pepper to Tate
- ½ lb. Red Potatoes, Cubed
- 1 Yellow Onion, Small & copped
- 1 Jalapeno, Small & Chopped
- 2 Ounces Ham, Cubed
- Pinch Mesquite Seasoning
- Pinch Chili Powder
- Pinch Taco Seasoning
- 1 Small Avocado, Pitted, Peeled & Chopped
- Salsa for Serving
- 2 Tortillas
- 1 Cup + 1 Tablespoon Water

Directions:

1. Mix your salt, pepper, mesquite seasoning, eggs, chili powder, taco seasoning and a tablespoon of water together.
2. Add in your potatoes, hams, onion and jalapeno into a dish, pouring everything else into it.
3. Fill your instant pot with a cup of water, and then add in your trivet. Cover, cooking for thirteen minutes on high heat. Use a quick release for the remaining pressure.
4. Divide between two tortillas and add in salsa and avocado to serve.

Peach Breakfast

Serves: 2

Time: 15 Minutes

Ingredients:

- 2 Cups Water
- ½ Peach, Chopped
- 1 Cup Rolled Oats
- ½ Teaspoon Vanilla Extract, Pure
- 3 Tablespoons Almonds, Chopped
- 1 Tablespoon Flax Meal
- Maple Syrup to Taste

Directions:

1. Mix your oat, water, vanilla extract and peach together in your instant pot. Stir well.
2. Cover, cooking on high pressure for three minutes. Use a quick release.
3. Stir, and then divide between two bowls. Top with almonds, flax meal and maple syrup before serving.

Easy Banana Bread

Serves: 2

Time: 1 Hour

Ingredients:

- ½ Tablespoons Vanilla
- ½ Stick Butter, Soft
- 2 Bananas, Peeled & Mashed
- ¼ Cup Sugar
- 1 Cup Flour
- 1 Egg
- ½ Teaspoon Baking Powder
- 1 Cup Water

Directions:

1. In a bowl mix your banana puree, vanilla, butter, sugar, flour, baking powder and egg together. Stir until well combined.
2. Grease a loaf pan, and then pour your batter in.
3. Add your water into your instant pot before putting your trivet in, and then place your loaf pan on the trivet. Cover, cooking on high pressure for fifty minutes before using a quick release.
4. Serve immediately or allow it to cool.

Vegetable Casserole

Serves: 2

Time: 40 Minutes

Ingredients:

- 3 Tablespoons Milk
- 3 Eggs
- 3 Tablespoons Flour
- Sea Salt & Black Pepper to Taste
- 1 Red Bell Pepper, Chopped
- ½ Cup Tomatoes, Chopped
- 1 Green Onion, Chopped
- ½ Cup Cheddar Cheese, Shredded
- 1 Zucchini, Small & Chopped
- 1 Cup Water

Directions:

1. Mix your flour, milk, eggs, salt, pepper, tomatoes, onion, bell pepper, zucchini and half of your cheese into a bowl. Stir well.
2. Pour the mixture into a heatproof dish, and then cover with tin foil.
3. Place your water into your instant pot, adding in your trivet. Put your vegetable ix in, and cover. Cook on high pressure for a half hour before using a quick release.
4. Uncover, and sprinkle with the remaining cheese before serving.

Blueberry Breakfast

Serves: 2

Time: 12 Minutes

Ingredients:

- 2/3 Cup Almond Milk
- 2/3 Cup Greek Yogurt
- 2/3 Cup Old Fashioned Oats
- 2/3 Cup Blueberries
- 1 Teaspoon Sugar
- 2 Tablespoons Chia Seeds
- Pinch of Cinnamon
- ½ Teaspoon Vanilla Extract, Pure
- 1 ½ Cups Water

Directions:

1. Mix your oat, milk, blueberries, yogurt, chia seeds, sugar, vanilla and cinnamon in a heatproof bowl.
2. Pour your water into the instant pot, adding it to your trivet. Place the bowl into your instant pot, and cook on high pressure for six minutes before using a quick release.
3. Stir in your blueberries, mixing again before serving.

Bacon Breakfast Potatoes

Serves: 2

Time: 18 Minutes

Ingredients:

- 1 Teaspoon Parsley, Dried
- 1 Bacon Strip, Chopped
- ½ lb. Red Potatoes, Cubed
- Sea Salt & Black Pepper to Taste
- 1.5 Ounces Cheddar Cheese, Grated
- ½ Teaspoon Garlic Powder
- 1 Ounce Ranch Dressing
- 1 Tablespoon Water

Directions:

1. Place your potatoes, bacon, parsley, salt, pepper, garlic, and water. Stir, and then cover. Cook on manual pressure for seven minutes before using a quick release.
2. Add in your dressing and cheese. Toss before serving.

Spanish Frittata

Serves: 2

Time: 30 Minutes

Ingredients:

- 1 Garlic Clove, Minced
- 2 Tablespoons Scallions, Chopped
- 2 Ounces Hash browns
- ½ Tablespoon Butter, Melted
- 3 Eggs
- Sea Salt & Black Pepper to Taste
- 2 Tablespoons Milk
- 1 Tablespoon Bisquick
- ½ Teaspoon Tomato Paste
- 1 ½ Cups Water
- 2 Ounces Cheddar Cheese, Grated

Directions:

1. Mix your milk, tomato paste and Bisquick together in a bowl and stir.
2. Get out another bowl, mixing your garlic, eggs, scallion, milk mix, and season with salt and pepper. Whisk well.
3. Spread your hash browns into a greased baking dish, adding in your melted butter. Pour your egg mix over everything.
4. Spread it out, and top with cheese.
5. Put your water into the instant pot before adding in your trivet.
6. Add your casserole dish inside, and over and cook for twenty minutes on high pressure before using a quick release.
7. Serve warm.

Squash Porridge

Serves: 2

Time: 20 Minutes

Ingredients:

- 2 Tablespoons Slippery Elm
- 1 ½ Tablespoons Gelatin
- 1 Small Delicata Squash
- 3 Apples, Small & Cored
- ½ Cup Water
- 1 ½ Tablespoons Maple Syrup
- Pinch Cinnamon Powder
- Pinch Ginger Powder
- Pinch Cloves, Ground

Directions:

1. Place your apples and squash into your instant pot before adding your cinnamon, ginger, cloves and water. Cover and cook for eight minutes before using a quick release.
2. Allow it to cool, transferring it to a cutting board. Halve and deseed your squash, transferring it to the blender.
3. Add in your water, apples and spices, pulsing well.
4. Add in your maple syrup, gelatin, and slippery elm, blending well.
5. Serve immediately.

Easy Oatmeal

Serves: 2

Time: 15 Minutes

Ingredients:

- 1 Teaspoon Vanilla Extract
- 1 ½ Cups Waters
- ½ Cup Steel Cut Oats

Directions:

1. Place your water in the instant pot, and then add in your vanilla and oats stir, and then cover.
2. Cook on high pressure for three minutes. Before allowing a natural pressure release for five minutes. Use a quick release for the remaining pressure.
3. Divide into two bowls and serve warm.

Easy Quinoa

Serves: 2

Time: 12 Minutes

Ingredients:

- Pinch Cinnamon
- ¼ Teaspoon Vanilla Extract
- 1 Tablespoon Maple Syrup
- 1 Cup Quinoa
- 2 Cups Water
- ¼ Cup Berries, Fresh

Directions:

1. Start by placing your quinoa into your instant pot, adding maple, water, cinnamon, and vanilla. Stir well, and cover.
2. Cook on high pressure for one minute. Allow for a natural pressure release for ten minutes before using a quick release for the remaining pressure. Fluff with a fork.
3. Serve with fresh berries.

Buckwheat Porridge

Serves: 2

Time: 17 Minutes

Ingredients:

- 1 Cup Buckwheat Groats, Rinsed
- 3 Cups Rice Milk
- ¼ Cup Raisins
- ½ Teaspoon Vanilla Extract, Pure
- 1 Banana, Peeled & Sliced

Directions:

1. Place your buckwheat into the instant pot, adding in your vanilla, banana, milk and raisins.
2. Stir, cover, and cook on high pressure for six minutes before using a quick release.
3. Serve warm.

Breakfast Cake

Serves: 2

Time: 35 Minutes

Ingredients:

- 3 Eggs
- 1 Cup Water
- 1 Tablespoon Butter, Melted
- 2 Tablespoons Sugar
- 5 Tablespoons Yogurt
- 5 Tablespoons Ricotta Cheese
- 1 Teaspoon Vanilla Extract, Pure
- 1 Teaspoon Baking Powder
- ½ Cup Whole Wheat Flour
- ½ Cup Berry Compote

Directions:

1. Mix your sugar and eggs together, whisking until the sugar dissolves.
2. Add in our butter, vanilla, ricotta cheese and yogurt. Mix well.
3. Get out another bowl and mix your baking powder and flour together. Stir it into your egg mixture, and then grease a cake pan. Pour in the batter, making sure it's spread evenly.
4. Drop spoonsful of your berry compote into the batter, and then swirl using a knife.
5. Add your water into your instant pot, putting your trivet inside. Place your cake pan in the trivet, and cover.
6. Cook on high pressure for twenty-five minutes, before using a quick release. Serve warm.

Pumpkin Oatmeal

Serves: 2

Time: 15 Minutes

Ingredients:

- ½ Teaspoon Cinnamon
- ½ Cup Pumpkin Puree
- ½ Cup Steel Cut Oats
- 2 Cups Water
- ½ Teaspoon Allspice
- ½ Teaspoon Vanilla Extract

Topping:

- 2 Tablespoons Pecans, Chopped
- 3 Tablespoons Brown Sugar
- ½ Tablespoon Cinnamon

Directions:

1. Put your water in the instant pot, and then add in your pumpkin puree, a half teaspoon cinnamon, allspice, steel cut oats, and vanilla. Stir well before covering, and cook on high pressure for three minutes before using a quick release.
2. In a bowl, mix your brown sugar, another half a tablespoon of cinnamon and pecans.
3. Divide your pumpkin oatmeal between bowls, and add your toppings before serving.

Sweet Potato Hash

Serves: 2

Time: 32 Minutes

Ingredients:

- 1 Cup Sweet Potato, Peeled & Cubed
- 1 Small Onion, Chopped
- 2 Tablespoons Olive Oil
- 2 Bacon Slices, Cooked & Chopped
- 1 Jalapeno Pepper, Chopped
- 2 Tablespoons Cilantro, Fresh & Chopped
- 2 Eggs
- Sea Salt & Black Pepper to Taste

Directions:

1. Grease a casserole dish before putting it aside.
2. Put your sweet potato in the casserole dish, and then fill your instant pot with one and a half cups water. Place your trivet in your instant pot, and then place your casserole dish on your trivet.
3. Cook on high pressure for eight minutes, and then use a quick release.
4. Allow it to cool, and then drain the water. Dry your instant pot.
5. Put your oil in the instant pot, and then press sauté. Add in your onion, cooking for four to five minutes.
6. Add in sweet potato and all of your ingredients except for your eggs.
7. Make two wells in the potato mixture, and then crack an egg in each.
8. Press cancel, and then close your lid.
9. Allow it to cool for ten minutes before serving.

Lunch Recipes

Lunch is an important part of the day, and there's no reason to skip it. These lunches are delicious and easy to heat up!

Potato & Beef Stew

Serves: 2
Time: 1 Hour 5 Minutes
Ingredients:

- ½ lb. Beef Stew Meat, Cubed
- 1 Tablespoon Olive Oil
- 1 Onion, Small & Chopped
- 2 Potatoes, Chopped
- 2 Carrots, Peeled & Chopped
- 1 Celery Stalk, Chopped
- 1 ½ Cups Beef Broth
- 1 Cup Kale Leaves, Trimmed & Chopped
- ½ Teaspoon Garlic Powder
- 1 Tablespoon Hot Sauce
- Sea Salt & Black Pepper to Taste

Directions:

1. Press sauté and add in your oil. Cook your beef until browned. It should take about four to five minutes. Press cancel before adding in your remaining ingredients.
2. Press your meat/stew setting, and then use a quick release when done. Serve warm.

Butterfly Pasta

Serves: 2

Time: 10 Minutes

Ingredients:

- 16 Ounces Farfalle Pasta
- 2 Cloves Garlic, Smashed
- ½ Teaspoon Oregano
- 2 Hot Chili Peppers, Chopped
- ½ Teaspoon Oregano
- 2 Cups Tomato Puree
- 1 Tablespoon Olive Oil
- Sea Salt & Black Pepper to Taste

Directions:

1. Press sauté, and heat up your oil. Once your oil begins to shimmer, add in your garlic. Cook until your garlic lightly browns.
2. Add in your remaining ingredients along with enough water to cover the pasta. Press cancel, and then cook on manual for four minutes.
3. Use a quick release, and serve warm.

Pork Burritos

Serves: 2

Time: 30 Minutes

Ingredients:

- 4 Ounces Ground Pork
- Sea Salt & Black Pepper to Taste
- ½ Teaspoon Sage
- ½ Teaspoon Thyme
- ½ Teaspoon Brown Sugar
- ½ Teaspoon Fennel Seeds
- ¼ Teaspoon Nutmeg
- ¼ Teaspoon Red Pepper Flakes
- 1 Cup + ½ Tablespoon Water
- 4 Tortilla Shells
- 4 Eggs
- 2 Tablespoons Milk
- 2 Tablespoons Olive Oil
- Cheddar Cheese, Shredded for Garnish
- Salsa for Serving

Directions:

1. Mix your pork, salt, pepper, thyme, sage, pepper flakes, fennel, nutmeg, sugar and a half a tablespoon of water. Stir well.
2. Brush your tortilla shells down with olive oil before placing them on the baking sheet, and then cover them with tin foil. Make sure to seal the edges.
3. Get out a heat proof dish, and then mix your salt, pepper, milk, eggs, and meat. Stir well before covering them with tin foil.
4. Add in your remaining water to the instant pot before placing your steamer basket in. put your heatproof dish on your steamer basket, and add in your wrapped tortilla shells on top.
5. Cook on high pressure for fifteen minutes.
6. Unwrap your tortilla shells, and stuff them with your meat mixture.
7. Top with your cheddar and salsa before serving.

Tuna Casserole

Serves: 2

Time: 15 Minutes

Ingredients:

- 2 Cans Tuna
- 2 ½ Cups Macaroni Pasta
- 3 Cups Water
- 1 Cup Peas, Frozen
- 1 Can Cream of Mushroom Soup
- 1 Cup Cheddar Cheese, Shredded
- Sea Salt & Black Pepper to Taste

Directions:

1. Mix your soup in with your water, placing it in the instant pot. Add all ingredients except for cheese.
2. Cook on high pressure for four minutes, and then use a quick release.
3. Sprinkle your cheese on top, and allow it to melt and sauce to thicken before serving.

Zucchini Soup

Serves: 2

Time: 40 Minutes

Ingredients:

- 1 Onion, Chopped Rough
- 2 Tablespoons Olive oil
- 2 Cloves Garlic, Crushed
- 2 Potatoes, Small ½ Cubes
- 2 Carrots, Cut into ½ Slices
- 4 Zucchinis, Cut into Slices
- Sea Salt & Black Pepper to Taste
- 4 Cups Vegetable Stock
- 1 Tablespoon Basil, Fresh

Directions:

1. Press sauté, and then add in your oil.
2. Once your oil is heated add in your garlic and onions, sautéing for a minute.
3. Add in your potatoes, cooking for another two to three minutes.
4. Add all remaining ingredients, stirring to blend.
5. Cook on high pressure for five minutes.
6. Use a quick release, and season with salt and pepper to taste. Serve warm.

Salmon Casserole

Serves: 2

Time: 25 Minutes

Ingredients:

- 2 Cups Peas & Corn Mix
- 2 Salmon Fillets, Boneless
- 2 Cups Milk
- 1 Teaspoon Garlic, Minced
- ¼ Cup Olive Oil
- Sea Salt & Black Pepper to Tate
- 2 Cups Chicken Stock
- ¼ Teaspoon Dill, Fresh & Chopped
- ¼ Teaspoon Cilantro, Chopped
- 1 Tablespoon Parmesan, Grated
- 4 Ounces Cream of Celery Soup

Directions:

1. Add your oil in, and press sauté. Allow it to heat up, and add in your salmon. Cook for a couple of minutes.
2. Add in your garlic and chicken. Flake your salmon, and stir well.
3. Add in your cream of celery, peas, corn, dill, milk, cilantro, salt and pepper. Stir well, and then cook on high pressure for eight minutes.
4. Use a quick release, sprinkling with parmesan before serving.

Cabbage Rolls

Serves: 2

Time: 50 Minutes

Ingredients:

- ½ Cup Brown Rice
- ½ Tablespoon Olive Oil
- 4 Cups Water
- 1 ½ Cups Mushrooms, Chopped
- ½ Yellow Onion, Chopped
- 1 Clove Garlic, Minced
- Sea Salt & Black Pepper to Taste
- 6 Green Cabbage Leaves
- ½ Teaspoon Walnuts, Chopped
- ½ Teaspoon Caraway Seeds
- ¼ Teaspoon Cayenne Pepper

Directions:

1. Place two cups of water and rice into your instant pot. Cook on high pressure for fifteen minutes before using a quick release. Drain your rice before transferring it to a bowl.
2. Heat up a pan with oil using medium-high heat. Add in your onion, garlic, walnuts, mushrooms, caraway, salt, pepper and cayenne. Cook for five minutes before adding in your rice. Make sure to stir well.
3. Place the rest of your water into a pot, bringing it to a boil. Balance your cabbage leaves for one minute, and then drain them.
4. Divide your rice mixture into the middle, rolling and sealing the edges.
5. Transfer these rolls into your instant pot, adding water to cover them.
6. Cook on high pressure for ten minutes, and use a quick release afterwards. Serve warm.

Sausage & Bell Peppers

Serves: 2

Time: 35 Minutes

Ingredients:

- 5 Sausages, Sliced
- 2 Green Bell Peppers, Sliced into Strips
- 6 Ounces Tomato Sauce
- 14 Ounces Tomatoes, Canned & Chopped
- ½ Cup Water
- ½ Tablespoon Basil, Fresh & Chopped
- 1 Teaspoon Garlic Powder
- ½ Tablespoon Italian Seasoning

Directions:

1. Mix everything together in your instant pot, and cook on high pressure for twenty-five minutes.
2. Use a quick release, and serve warm.

Beef Sandwiches

Serves: 2

Time: 50 Minutes

Ingredients:

- ½ lb. Brown Sugar
- 1 lb. Beef Roast, Chunked
- ½ Teaspoon Smoked Paprika
- 1 Teaspoon Garlic Powder
- Sea Salt & Black Pepper to Taste
- ½ Teaspoon Mustard Powder
- ½ Teaspoon Onion Flakes
- 2 Teaspoons Balsamic Vinegar
- 1 Cup Beef Stock
- ½ Tablespoon Worcestershire Sauce
- 1 Tablespoon Butter, Melted
- 2 Cheddar Cheese Slices
- 2 Hoagie Rolls

Directions:

1. Place your meat in the instant pot, seasoning with garlic, salt, pepper, paprika, mustard powder, onion flakes, and then ad in your Worcestershire sauce, stock and vinegar. Stir well.
2. Cook on high pressure for forty minutes, and then use a quick release.
3. Shred your meat, and then divide it between your two rolls after buttering them.
4. Place your cheese on each, and then heat your broiler. Broil for a few more minutes, and serve with some cooking liquid on the side for dipping.

Chicken Sandwiches

Serves: 2

Time: 25 Minutes

Ingredients:

- 3 Ounces Orange Juice, Canned
- 2 Chicken Breasts, Skinless & Boneless
- 1 Tablespoon Lemon Juice, Fresh
- 4 Ounces Peaches, Canned with Juices
- ½ Teaspoon Soy Sauce
- 2 Teaspoons Cornstarch
- 7 Ounces Pineapple, Canned & Chopped
- 1 Tablespoon Brown Sugar
- 2 Hamburger Buns
- 2 Pineapple Slices, Grilled

Directions:

1. Mix your orange juice, soy sauce, pineapples, peaches, sugar, and lemon juice. Put half of this mix in your instant pot and add in your chicken. Put the rest of the orange juice in, and then cook on high pressure for twenty minutes.
2. Shred your chicken.
3. Place your chicken in a bowl, and in a different bowl mix a tablespoon of cooking juices with your cornstarch.
4. Place this slurry in your pot, returning your chicken to the instant pot. Press sauté, cooking for four to five minutes.
5. Divide between buns and top with grilled pineapple to serve.

Bean Chili

Serves: 2

Time: 1 Hour 5 Minutes

Ingredients:

- ½ Cup Mixed Red, Yellow & Orange Bell Peppers, Chopped
- 1 Yellow Onion, Chopped
- ½ lb. Ground Beef
- 3 Cloves Garlic, Minced
- 2 Cups Kidney Beans
- 6 Ounces Canned Tomatoes, Chopped
- ½ Tablespoon Honey, Raw
- 2 Teaspoons Cocoa Powder
- Sea Salt & Black Pepper to Taste
- 1 Teaspoon Sweet Paprika
- 1 Teaspoon Coriander
- 1 ½ Tablespoons Chili Powder
- ½ Tablespoon Cumin

Directions:

1. Press sauté, and then add your beef in. allow it to brown while stirring.
2. Add in your bell pepper and onion, stirring well. Cook for another two minutes.
3. Add in your beans, tomatoes, garlic, honey, cocoa powder, paprika, coriander, chili powder, cumin, salt and pepper. Cook on manual pressure for forty minutes.
4. Serve warm.

Apple & Squash Soup

Serves: 2

Time: 25 Minutes

Ingredients:

- ½ Butternut Squash, Peeled & Cubed
- Drizzle of Olive Oil
- Pinch of }Ginger Powder
- 1 Apple, Small, Peeled, Cored & Chopped
- 2 Cups Vegetable Stock
- Sea Salt to Taste
- White Pepper to Taste

Directions:

1. Put your oil in the instant pot, and press sauté. Allow it to heat up, and add in your squash cubes. Allow them to brown for five minutes.
2. Add ginger, apple, stock, salt and pepper. Stir, and then cook in high pressure for fifteen minutes.
3. Puree your soup with an immersion blender, and divide between two bowls.

Chicken Wrap

Serves: 2

Time: 20 Minutes

Ingredients:

- 2 Teaspoons Garlic, Minced
- 1 Yellow Onion, Chopped
- ½ lb. Chicken, Ground
- Pinch Ginger, Grated
- Pinch Allspice
- 2 Tablespoons Soy Sauce
- 4 Tablespoons Water Chestnuts
- 2 Tablespoon Chicken Stock
- 2 Tortillas for Serving
- 2 Tablespoons Balsamic Vinegar

Directions:

1. Mix your chicken, onion, ginger, garlic, chestnuts, allspice, stock, vinegar, and soy sauce. Stir, and cook on manual for ten minutes
2. Divide between tortillas before serving warm.

Carrot Soup

Serves: 2

Time: 40 Minutes

Ingredients:

- 1 Onion, Small & Chopped
- 1 Tablespoon Butter, Unsalted
- ½ Teaspoon Ginger, Fresh & Minced
- 1 Clove Garlic, Minced
- ½ lb. Carrots, Peeled & Chopped
- Sea Salt & Black Pepper to Taste
- 7 Ounces Coconut Milk, Canned & Unsweetened
- 1 Cup Chicken Broth
- 1/8 Teaspoon Brown Sugar
- ½ Tablespoon Sriracha
- 1 Tablespoon Cilantro, Fresh & Chopped

Directions:

1. Put your butter in your instant pot before pressing sauté. Add in your onion, cooking for three minutes.
2. Add your garlic and ginger, cooking for another minute.
3. Add in your carrots, seasoning with salt and pepper. Cook for another two minutes.
4. Press cancel before adding in your coconut milk, Sriracha and broth, and stir well.
5. Secure the lid, cooking on high pressure for six minutes.
6. Use a natural pressure release for ten minutes, and then use a quick release for any remaining pressure.
7. Remove the lid adding in your brown sugar. Stir well.
8. Use an immersion blender to puree your soup, and garnish with cilantro before serving.

Fried Rice

Serves: 2

Time: 15 Minutes

Ingredients:

- 1 Carrot
- 1 Cup Long Grain Rice
- 1 ¼ Cup Vegetable Broth
- 1 ½ Tablespoons Olive Oil
- 1 Egg
- ¼ Cup Peas, Frozen
- Sea Salt & Black Pepper to Taste

Directions:

1. Put your rice and vegetable stock in your instant pot, and make sure it's spread out evenly. Dice your carrot before adding it in.
2. Seal your instant pot, and then cook on high pressure for three minutes.
3. Allow it to sit for two to three minutes with a natural pressure release before using a quick release.
4. Mix your rice, and then press sauté.
5. Add in your oil and frozen peas, sautéing for another minute.
6. Make a well in your rice, and then beat your eggs in a bowl.
7. Pour your beaten eggs in, and fry everything together for two minutes.
8. Season with salt and black pepper. Serve warm.

Minestrone Soup

Serves: 2

Time: 20 Minutes

Ingredients:

- 1 Bay Leaf
- 1 Tablespoon Olive Oil
- 1 Onion, Diced
- Sea Salt & Black Pepper to Taste
- ¼ Cup Spinach, Fresh
- 2 Cups Chicken Broth
- ½ Cup Elbow Pasta
- 14 Ounces Tomatoes, Diced
- 1 Cup White Beans, Cooked
- 1 Teaspoon Bail
- 1 Teaspoon Oregano
- 1 Carrot, Diced
- 2 Cloves Garlic, Minced

Directions:

1. Press sauté, and then add in your oil and carrot. Next, add in your garlic, celery and onion. Cook until your onion softens.
2. Add in your basil, pepper, salt and oregano, mixing well.
3. Add in your broth, pasta, bay leaf, spinach and tomatoes. Press cancel.
4. Cook on high pressure for six minutes, and allow for a natural pressure release for five minutes. Use a quick release for any remaining pressure.
5. Open the lid, adding in your beans. Serve warm.

Black Bean Curry

Serves: 2

Time: 50 Minutes

Ingredients:

- 1 Tablespoon Olive Oil
- 1 Teaspoon Cumin Seeds
- 1 Onion, Chopped
- 1 Tablespoon Garlic Paste
- 1 Tablespoon Ginger Paste
- 2 Teaspoon Corianders
- 1 Teaspoon Red Chili Powder
- ½ Teaspoon Turmeric
- 1 Cup Black Beans, Soaked Overnight & Drained
- 2 Cups Water
- ½ Teaspoon Garam Masala
- 1 Teaspoon Lemon Juice, Fresh
- Sea Salt to Taste

Directions:

1. Put your oil in your instant pot and press sauté. Add in your cumin seeds, cooking for half a minute.
2. Add in your garlic, spices, ginger and onion, cooking for three to four more minutes.
3. Press cancel, and stir in your water and beans. Secure the lid, and then press the bean/chili option.
4. Cook for thirty minutes before using a natural pressure release.
5. Stir in your lemon juice before serving hot.

Asparagus Risotto

Serves: 2

Time: 15 Minutes

Ingredients:

- 1 Clove Garlic, Minced
- 1 Tablespoon Olive Oil
- ½ Brown Onion, Dice Fine
- ¼ Fennel, Diced
- ¼ Bunch Asparagus, Diced
- ¼ Teaspoon Sea Salt Fine
- ½ Lemon, Zested
- 1/6 Cup White Wine
- 1 Cup Arborio Risotto Rice
- 1 Cup Vegetable Stock
- 1 Cup Chicken Stock
- ¼ Cup Parmesan Cheese
- 1 Tablespoon Butter
- ½ Fennel, Sliced for Garnish
- ½ Tablespoon Olive Oil for Topping
- Sea Salt for Topping

Directions:

1. Start by pressing your sauté button, and then add in your onions and olive oil. Cook until the onions are tender.
2. Prepare your vegetables, dicing them as desired.
3. Add in ¾ of your asparagus and fennel before seasoning with salt and garlic. Mix well.
4. Add in your white wine, rice and lemon zest, stirring until well combined.
5. Add in your stock, stirring and press the keep warm button.
6. Put the lid on, and then cook for five minutes on high pressure.
7. Heat a tablespoon of oil in a frying pan, placing it over medium-high heat while your risotto is cooking. Cook your remaining asparagus and fennel, cooking for five minutes. Cook until golden brown, drizzling with lemon juice before placing it to the side.
8. Allow for a natural pressure release for two minutes before using a quick release for the remaining pressure.
9. Open the lid, and stir in your cheese and butter. Season, and top with your fennel and asparagus.

Pork Soup

Serves: 2
Time: 50 Minutes
Ingredients:

- 1 Onion, Small & Chopped
- 1 Cup Carrot, Peeled & Shredded
- ½ lb. Ground Pork
- 1 Tablespoon Olive Oil
- 1 ½ Cups Cabbage, Shopped
- 2 Cups Chicken Broth, Low Sodium
- 1 Tablespoon Soy Sauce
- ½ Teaspoon Ground Ginger
- Black Pepper to Taste

Directions:

1. Put your oil in your instant pot before pressing sauté.
2. Add in your pork, cooking until browned. This should take about five minutes. Press cancel, and stir in all of your remaining ingredients.
3. Secure the lid, cooking on high pressure for twenty-five minutes.
4. Use a quick release, and serve warm.

Easy Chicken Chili

Serves: 2
Time: 35 Minutes
Ingredients:

- 1 Tablespoon Olive Oil
- 6 Ounces Chicken Breasts, Boneless, Skinless & Cubed
- 1 Onion, Small & Chopped
- 2 Cloves Garlic, Minced
- ½ Sweet Potato, Peeled & Cubed
- 1 Jalapeno Pepper, Chopped
- ½ Teaspoon Oregano
- ½ Teaspoon Cumin
- 1 Tablespoon Red Chili Powder
- 8 Ounces Black Beans, Canned, Drained & Rinsed
- 8 Ounces Tomatoes, Canned, Diced & Drained
- ¼ Cup Quinoa, Uncooked
- 1 ¾ Cup Chicken Broth
- 1 Tablespoon Lemon Juice, Fresh
- Sea Salt & Black Pepper to Taste

Directions:

1. Put your oil in your instant pot, and press sauté. Add in your chicken cooking for four to five minutes.
2. Use a slotted spoon to transfer your chicken to a bowl before setting it to the side.
3. Add your sweet potato and onion to the pot, cooking for five minutes.
4. Add in your jalapeno pepper, oregano, spices and garlic, cooking for another minute.
5. Press cancel, and stir. Cook your chicken and remaining ingredients together except for your lemon juice.
6. Secure the lid, cooking on high pressure for four minutes.
7. Use a natural pressure release for ten minutes, and then use a quick release for any remaining pressure.
8. Serve war and drizzled with lemon juice.

Easy Goulash

Serves: 2
Time: 10 Minutes
Ingredients:

- ½ lb. Ground Beef
- 2 Cloves Garlic, Minced
- 1 Onion, Small
- 15 Ounces Tomato Sauce, Canned
- 15 ounces Diced Tomatoes, Canned
- 1 ½ Cups Elbow Noodles
- 1 ½ Tablespoons Soy Sauce
- 2 Bay Leaves
- 1 Tablespoon Italian Seasoning
- 1 ¼ Cup Water
- Sea Salt & Black Pepper to Taste

Directions:

1. Press sauté on your instant pot, and then add in your onion, garlic, ground beef, and season with salt and pepper. Cook until your ground beef is browned.
2. Once it's browned, drain the fat, and then add in your tomato sauce, diced tomatoes, and Italian seasoning. Stir before adding in your water, noodles, soy sauce and bay leaves.
3. Put your instant pot on manual, cooking on high pressure for four minutes. Use a quick release and take your bay leaves out. Stir well before serving.

Snack & Appetizers

When you're looking for something a little extra, you can pull these recipes out for a fun filled day! They're great if you want to relax with family night on the weekends.

Jalapeno Bean Dip

Serves: 2

Time: 40 Minutes

Ingredients:

- 2 Cloves Garlic, Chopped
- 1 Jalapeno, Seeded
- ½ Teaspoon Paprika
- 1 Cup Pinto Beans, Dried Rinsed
- ½ Teaspoon Chili Powder
- ½ Teaspoon Cumin
- 1 Onion, Quartered
- ¼ Cup Salsa
- ½ Teaspoon Sea Salt, Fine
- ¼ Teaspoon Black Pepper
- 1 ½ Cups Water

Directions:

1. Throw all of your ingredients into your instant pot and stir.
2. Cook on high pressure for twenty-eight minutes, and then use a quick release.
3. Use an immersion blender to blend until smooth, and serve with tortilla chips.

Pumpkin Granola

Serves: 2

Time: 35 Minutes

Ingredients:

- ½ Tablespoon Butter
- 1 ½ Cups Water
- ½ Cup Pumpkin Puree
- ½ Cup Steel Cut Oats
- 2 Tablespoons Maple Syrup
- ½ Teaspoon Pumpkin Pie Spice
- 1 Teaspoon Cinnamon

Directions:

1. Press sauté, and then melt your butter.
2. Once your butter is melted, add in oats, and stir well. Cook for three minutes.
3. Add in your remaining ingredients, and cook on high pressure for ten minutes.
4. Use a quick release, and serve room temperature.

Mango Salsa

Serves: 2

Time: 35 Minutes

Ingredients:

- 2 Teaspoons Olive Oil
- ½ Shallot, Chopped
- ¼ Teaspoon Cinnamon
- 2 Teaspoon Ginger, Fresh & Grated
- 1 Red Hot Chili Pepper, Minced
- 1 Apple, Small, Peeled, Cored & Chopped
- 1 Mango, Peeled & Chopped
- Pinch Sea Salt
- 1 Tablespoon Raisins
- 2 Tablespoons White Wine
- 2 Tablespoons White Vinegar

Directions:

1. Press sauté, heating up your oil in your instant pot.
2. Once it's heated add your ginger, shallot, chili pepper, cardamom and cinnamon. Stir well and cook for two to three minutes.
3. Add in your remaining ingredients, and cook on high pressure for fifteen minutes.
4. Use a quick release and serve with tortilla chips.

Cauliflower Dip

Serves: 2

Time: 20 Minutes

Ingredients:

- ½ Cup Cauliflower Florets
- ¼ Teaspoon Onion Powder
- ½ Cup Water
- 1 Clove Garlic, Minced
- ¼ Teaspoon Mustard Powder
- ¼ Teaspoon Smoked Paprika
- ¼ Teaspoon Turmeric
- 1 Tablespoon Nutritional Yeast
- 2 Teaspoons Cornstarch
- 2 Teaspoons Chickpea Miso
- Sea Salt to Taste
- 2 Teaspoons Lemon Juice

Directions:

1. Place your cauliflower, garlic, paprika, water, turmeric and mustard in your instant pot. Stir and cook on high pressure for ten minutes.
2. Use a quick release, and transfer everything into your blender.
3. Blend well before serving.

BBQ Wings

Serves: 2
Time: 35 Minutes
Ingredients:

- 2 lb. Chicken Wings
- ½ Cup BBQ Sauce
- 1 Cup Water

Directions:

1. Put your water in your instant pot before adding your steamer basket. Place your chicken in your basket, and cook on high pressure for five minutes.
2. Place your BBQ sauce in a bowl, and toss your wings in after using a quick release.
3. Place them on a lined baking sheet, and heat your oven to 450.
4. Cook for eighteen minutes, and then serve warm.

Easy Meatballs

Serves: 2

Time: 40 Minutes

Ingredients:

- 1 Tablespoon Olive Oil
- ½ Yellow Onion, Chopped
- 1 Clove Garlic, Minced
- 7 Ounces Tomato Sauce
- ½ Cup Water
- ½ Tablespoon Worcestershire Sauce
- ½ lb. Ground Beef
- 4 Tablespoons Rice
- Sea Salt & Black Pepper to Taste

Directions:

1. Press sauté and then add in your oil. Let it heat up, and then add in half of your garlic and onion. Cook for four minutes, and then add in your Worcestershire sauce, water, and tomato sauce. Stir and bring it to a simmer.
2. In a bowl mix your rice, beef, salt, pepper, remaining onion and remaining garlic. Mix well and shape into meatballs. Add them into your instant pot.
3. Cook on high pressure for fifteen minutes, and then use a quick release.

Deviled Eggs

Serves: 2

Time: 20 Minutes

Ingredients:

- 2 Eggs, Large
- 1 Tablespoon Mayonnaise
- ½ Tablespoon Olive Oil
- ½ Teaspoon Dijon Mustard
- Dash of Sriracha
- ¼ Teaspoon Apple Cider Vinegar
- Paprika to Taste

Directions:

1. Add a cup of water into your instant pot before lowering in your steamer basket with your eggs inside.
2. Cook on high pressure for five minutes before using a quick release.
3. Transfer your eggs to cold water, allowing them to cool before peeling and halving them lengthwise.
4. Remove the yolks from the whites.
5. Mas your yolks with remaining ingredients except for your paprika.
6. Pipe this mixture back into your egg whites and sprinkle with paprika before serving.

Roasted Hummus

Serves: 2

Time: 1 Hour 40 Minutes

Ingredients:

- 3 Cups Water
- 1 Yellow Onion, Small & Chopped
- Pinch Sea Salt
- ½ lb. Garbanzo Beans
- 1 Tablespoon Olive Oil
- 2 Cloves Garlic, Minced
- Pinch Cumin
- 2 Tablespoons Lemon Juice, Fresh
- ½ Tablespoon Sesame Oil
- ½ Cup Sesame Seeds, Toasted

Directions:

1. Place your beans in your instant pot, adding in your water and salt. Cook on high pressure for one and a half hours.
2. Heat up a pan with oil over medium high heat, and add in your garlic and onion. Stir, cooking for two minutes.
3. Transfer your beans to a food processor, adding in all of your ingredients. Pulse until smooth.

Italian Dip

Serves: 2

Time: 1 Hour 5 Minutes

Ingredients:

- 1 lb. Beef Roast, Chunked
- 1 Tablespoon Italian Seasoning
- 4 Ounces Pepperoncini Peppers
- 2 Tablespoons Water
- 3 Ounces Beef Stock

Directions:

1. Mix all of your ingredients and cook on high pressure for fifty-five minutes.
2. Shred your meat, and stir well.

Chili Dip

Serves: 2

Time: 20 Minutes

Ingredients:

- 2 Ounces Red Chilies, Chopped
- 1 ½ Tablespoons Sugar
- 1.5 Ounces Bird's Eye Chilies, Chopped
- 5 Cloves Garlic, Minced
- 2 Ounces White Vinegar
- 2 Ounces Water

Directions:

1. Mix all of your ingredients except for your vinegar, cooking on high pressure for seven minutes.
2. Use a quick release, and then add in your vinegar.
3. Blend everything with an immersion blender, and sauté for ten minutes.
4. Serve with tortilla chips.

Old Bay Peanuts

Serves: 2

Time: 1 Hour

Ingredients:

- ½ lb. Raw Peanuts
- ½ Teaspoon Sea Salt, Fine
- 1 Teaspoon Old Bay Seasoning
- 2 Tablespoons Apple Cider Vinegar
- 1 Bay Leaf
- ½ Tablespoon Mustard Seed
- Water

Directions:

1. Rinse your peanuts using cold water. Make sure all twigs and roots are removed.
2. Add all of your ingredients into your instant pot, and cover your peanuts with water. Make sure to stir well.
3. Put a trivet on top of the peanuts, and then cook on high pressure for forty minutes. Use a natural pressure release, and then allow them to cool before serving.

Artichoke Spread

Serves: 2

Time: 30 Minutes

Ingredients:

- 1/2 lb. Artichokes, Cut Lengthwise
- ½ Cup Cannellini Beans, Soaked Overnight & Drained
- ½ Cup Water
- 1 Clove Garlic, Minced
- 2 Tablespoons Lemon Juice, Fresh
- 2 Tablespoons Greek Yogurt
- Sea Salt & Black Pepper to Taste

Directions:

1. Place your artichokes in a bowl adding in your lemon juice. Let it sit for fifteen minutes before adding them into the instant pot, adding in your beans.
2. Cook on high pressure for fifteen minutes, discarding the excess water.
3. Place your beans and artichokes in the blender, and blend them with remaining ingredients.

White Bean Dip

Serves: 2

Time: 25 Minutes

Ingredients:

- 1 Clove Garlic, Minced
- 1 ½ Tablespoons Lemon Juice, Fresh
- ½ Cup White Beans, Soaked Overnight & Drained
- 2 Tablespoons Olive Oil
- 1 Teaspoon Chili Powder
- 1 Teaspoon Cumin
- ¼ Teaspoon Red Pepper Flakes
- 1 ½ Tablespoons Cilantro, Fresh & Chopped
- Sea Salt & Black Pepper to Taste

Directions:

1. Place your beans in the instant pot, making sure they're covered with water. Cook on high pressure for thirteen minutes before using a quick release.
2. Drain your beans, transferring them into a food processor. Add all of your ingredients except for cilantro and pulse well.
3. Add cilantro and stir before serving.

Beefy Dip

Serves: 2

Time: 30 Minutes

Ingredients:

- ½ Cup Mushrooms, Chopped
- 2 Tablespoons Beer
- ½ Yellow Onion, Chopped
- ½ Teaspoon Garlic Powder
- 2 Ounces Cream Cheese
- ½ lb. Ground Beef
- ½ Tablespoon White Flour
- ½ Cup Cheddar Cheese, Shredded
- Sea Salt & Black Pepper to Taste

Directions:

1. Press sauté and heat up your oil. Add in your onion, mushrooms and beef. Stir well, allowing it to cook for five minutes.
2. Season with garlic, salt and pepper. Add in your beef, and cook on high pressure for ten minutes. Use a quick release.
3. Add in your flour and cream cheese. Press sauté, and cook for five more minutes.
4. Add in your cheese, making sure to toss until coated. Serve warm.

Applesauce

Serves: 2

Time: 15 Minutes

Ingredients:

- 1 Golden Apple, Large
- 1 Gala Apple, Large
- ½ Tablespoon Maple Syrup
- ¼ Teaspoon Cinnamon
- 1 Cup Water

Directions:

1. Core and peel your apples. Slice your apples thin, and then cut your slices into quarters. Put them in a large bowl.
2. Add in your maple syrup and cinnamon, making sure your apples are coated.
3. Place your water and apples in your instant pot.
4. Cook on high pressure for five minutes.
5. Allow for a natural pressure release for five minutes before using a quick release for any remaining pressure.
6. Break up any remaining chunks and store in the fridge. Allow it to cool before serving.

Red Pepper Dip

Serves: 2

Time: 2 Hours 10 Minutes

Ingredients:

- 2 Tablespoons Lemon Juice
- 2 Teaspoons Olive oil
- 1 Clove Garlic, Roasted
- 2 Tablespoons Sesame Seeds, Toasted
- 2 Red Bell Peppers
- 3 Cups Water
- ½ Teaspoon Sesame Oil
- 1/3 lb. Garbanzo Beans
- ¼ Teaspoon Cumin
- Sea Salt to Taste

Directions:

1. Place your beans in your instant pot, adding in your salt, water, and then cooking on high pressure for an hour and a half.
2. Transfer your beans to a bowl, making sure to reserve the cooking liquid.
3. Add in your water, adding in your steamer pot. Place your bell pepper inside, and cook on high pressure for fifteen minutes.
4. Peel your peppers, chopping them and placing them in a bowl.
5. Get out a pan and then put half of your sesame oil in it, heating it over medium-high heat. Add in your garlic and sesame seeds, stirring well. Cook for six minutes.
6. Blend everything together and serve with pita bread.

Dinner Recipes

Dinner can be hard for any parent, which is why your instant pot will become your best friend. These main dish recipes range from one pot dishes to the perfect meat to put on the table.

Garlic Pulled Pork

Serves: 2

Time: 50 Minutes

Ingredients:

- ¼ Teaspoon Sea Salt, Fine
- 1 Tablespoon Cornstarch
- 3 Tablespoons Water
- ½ Cup Onion, Chopped
- ½ Cup Beef Broth
- 1 lb. Pork Belly, Cubed
- 1 ½ Teaspoons Black Pepper
- 1 Teaspoon Thyme

Directions:

1. Place all of your ingredients except for your water and cornstarch.
2. Cook on high pressure for thirty-five minutes, and then use a quick release.
3. Combine your water and cornstarch, and then place it in your instant pot.
4. Allow it to simmer to thicken, and shred before serving.

Braised Cod

Serves: 2

Time: 10 Minutes

Ingredients:

- 1 Sprig Rosemary, Fresh
- 1 Cup White Wine
- 1 Teaspoon Oregano
- 1 lb. Cod, Cut into 4 Filets
- 1 Teaspoon Paprika
- 2 Cloves Garlic, Smashed
- 1 Cup Parsley, Fresh
- 10 Ounces Peas, Frozen

Directions:

1. Mix your spices, herbs, salt and wine together in a bowl, pouring it into your instant pot. Add in your peas.
2. Arrange your fish into your steamer basket, lowering it close to the liquid.
3. Cook on high pressure for five minutes, and then use a quick release.
4. Serve warm.

Jalapeno Shrimp

Serves: 2

Time: 15 Minutes

Ingredients:

- 1 Teaspoon White Pepper
- 1 Teaspoon Cayenne Pepper
- 2 Cloves Garlic, Minced
- 1 Sweet Onion, Minced
- 1 Jalapeno Pepper, Minced
- 15 Ounces Tomatoes, Diced & Canned
- 1 lb. Shrimp, Frozen, Peeled & Deveined
- 1 Lemon, Juiced
- 1 Teaspoon Black Pepper

Directions:

1. Your frozen shrimp should come to room temperature. This may take fifteen minutes, so prepare it in advance.
2. Throw in all of your ingredients into the instant pot, and then cook on high pressure for five minutes.
3. Use a quick release and serve warm.

Easy Chicken Pasta

Serves: 2

Time: 20 Minutes

Ingredients:

- ½ Teaspoon Olive Oil
- ½ Cup Red Bell Pepper, Diced
- ½ Cup Tomatoes, Diced
- ½ Teaspoon Oregano
- 1 Bay Leaf
- 1 ½ Cups Chicken, Diced
- ½ Cup Onion, Chopped
- ¼ Teaspoon Sea Salt, Fine
- ½ Teaspoon Black Pepper
- 2 Tablespoons Parsley, Chopped
- Cooked Pasta of Your Choice

Directions:

1. Press sauté and then add in your onion and oil, cooking for two minutes. It should soften
2. Add in your diced tomatoes, bell pepper and chicken. Season with salt, pepper, oregano, and add in your bay leaf.
3. Cook on high pressure for ten minutes, and then allow for a natural pressure release this should take about eight to ten minutes.
4. Top with parsley and serve over cooked pasta.

Caramel Salmon

Serves: 2

Time: 20 Minutes

Ingredients:

- 1 Tablespoon Fish Sauce
- 2 Tablespoons Brown Sugar
- 2 Tablespoons Soy Sauce
- ¾ lb. Salmon Fillets
- 1 Teaspoon Vegetable Oil
- 1 Tablespoon Lemon Juice
- ½ Teaspoon Ginger
- ¼ Teaspoon Black Pepper
- ¼ Teaspoon Lemon Zest

Directions:

1. Sprinkle your salmon with salt and pepper, and then get out a bowl. Mix your vegetable oil, fish sauce, brown sugar, soy sauce, lemon juice, ginger and lemon zest.
2. Press sauté, and then add in your oil. Allow it to heat up. Allow it to caramelize before adding in your salmon, and cook on high pressure for five minutes.
3. Use a natural pressure release, and serve warm.

Italian Mussels

Serves: 2

Time: 20 Minutes

Ingredients:

- 3 Tablespoons Onion, Chopped
- 1 Clove Garlic, Minced
- 1 Tablespoon Red Pepper Flakes
- 1 ½ lbs. Mussels, Scrubbed
- 20 Ounces Tomatoes, Canned & Chopped
- 2 Tablespoons Olive Oil
- 1 Jalapeno Pepper, Chopped
- 2 Tablespoons Balsamic Vinegar
- 2 Tablespoon White Wine
- 2 Tablespoons Basil, Chopped
- Pinch Sea Salt, Fine

Directions:

1. Press sauté, and then heat up your oil. Your oil should begin to shimmer when it's hot.
2. Add in your cinnamon, chili peppers, cardamom, shallot and ginger. Stir well and cook for three to four minutes. It should become fragrant.
3. Add all remaining ingredients, and then cook on high pressure for fifteen minutes.
4. Use a quick release, and serve warm.

Lamb Casserole

Serves: 2

Time: 45 Minutes

Ingredients:

- ½ lb. Baby Potatoes
- ½ lb. Rack of Lamb
- 1 Carrot, Chopped
- ½ Onion, Chopped
- 1 Celery Stalk, Chopped
- 1 Tomato, Chopped
- 1 Cup Chicken Stock
- Sea Salt & Black Pepper to Taste
- 2 Cloves Garlic, Minced
- 1 Teaspoon Sweet Paprika
- 1 Teaspoon Cumin
- ¼ Teaspoon Oregano, Dried
- ¼ Teaspoon Rosemary
- 1 Tablespoon Red Wine
- 1 Tablespoon Ketchup

Directions:

1. Add everything into your instant pot, and cook on manual for thirty-five minutes.
2. Serve warm.

Salmon with Chili Sauce

Serves: 2

Time: 15 Minutes

Ingredients:

- 2 Salmon Fillets
- Sea Salt & Black Pepper to Taste
- 1 Cup Water
- 1 Jalapeno, Chopped
- 2 Cloves Garlic, Minced
- 1 Lime, Juiced
- 1 Tablespoon Honey, Raw
- 1 Tablespoon Hot Water
- 1 Tablespoon Olive Oil
- 1 Tablespoon Parsley, Chopped
- ½ Teaspoon Cumin
- ½ Teaspoon Sweet Paprika

Directions:

1. Mix your lime juice, garlic, jalapeno, oil, a tablespoon of water, honey, paprika, cumin, and parsley together in a bowl. Whisk well before placing it to the side.
2. Add a cup of water into your instant pot before adding in your steamer basket. Place your salmon in the steamer basket, seasoning with salt and pepper.
3. Steam for five minutes.
4. Divide between two plates, and drizzle with your sauce.

Jambalaya

Serves: 2

Time: 35 Minutes

Ingredients:

- ½ Tablespoon Olive Oil
- 1/3 lb. Chicken Breasts, Chopped
- 1/3 lb. Shrimp
- ½ Cup Bell Pepper, Chopped
- ½ Cup Yellow Onion, Chopped
- ½ Tablespoon Garlic, Minced
- 2 Cups Chicken Stock
- ½ Cup Rice
- ½ Cup Tomatoes, Crushed
- 2 Teaspoons Creole Seasoning
- 2 Teaspoons Worcestershire Sauce
- 1/3 lb. Sausage, Cooked & Sliced

Directions:

1. Add your oil into your instant pot, and press sauté.
2. Allow it to heat up, and add your chicken in. sprinkle half of your creole seasoning over your chicken, and toss to coat. Brown your chicken for a few minutes per side.
3. Place your chicken in a bowl before adding your bell pepper, onion and garlic into your instant pot. Cook for two minutes.
4. Add in your rice, stirring well. Cook for two more minutes.
5. Throw in the rest of your creole seasoning, tomato, Worcestershire sauce and chicken. Cook on the rice setting.
6. Add in your shrimp and sausage, cooking for two more minutes.
7. Serve warm.

Salmon Risotto

Serves: 2

Time: 25 Minutes

Ingredients:

- 2 Salmon Fillets, Boneless
- 1/3 Lemon, Juiced
- 1 ½ Cups Water

Rice:

- 1 Yellow Onion, Chopped
- 12 Ounces Mushrooms, Sliced
- 1 Cup Artichokes, Chopped
- 1 Cup Arborio Rice
- ½ Tablespoon Garlic, Minced
- 2 Tablespoons White Wine
- 2 Cups Chicken Stock
- 1 Teaspoon Olive Oil
- ½ Cup Parmesan, Grated

Directions:

1. Place your water in the instant pot, and then add in your steamer basket. Place your fish inside, and drizzle your fresh lemon juice over it. Steam for three minutes, and then divide between two plates, setting your fish to the side for now.
2. Clean out your instant pot, and then add in your oil. Press sauté, and then add in your onion, garlic and mushrooms. Cook for three minutes, and don't forget to stir.
3. Add in your wine, ice, stock, and artichokes. Cook on manual for seven minutes.
4. Add in your parmesan, and stir. Divide between your plates, and serve with salmon.

Pineapple Pork Delight

Serves: 2
Time: 1 Hour 50 Minutes
Ingredients:

- 1 Tablespoon Olive Oil
- 1 lb. Pork, Cubed
- Sea Salt & Black Pepper to Taste
- 2 Tablespoons Cassava Flour
- ½ Tablespoon Soy Sauce
- Pinch Cloves
- Pinch Turmeric Powder
- Pinch Ginger Powder
- 1 Yellow Onion, Small & Sliced Thick
- 1 Garlic Clove, Minced
- ½ Teaspoon Cinnamon
- ½ Cup Pineapple, Peeled & Chopped into Chunks
- 1 Tablespoon Dates, Pitted & Chopped
- 1 Bay Leaves
- ½ Cup Beef Stock
- ½ Bunch Swiss Chard, Chopped

Directions:

1. Mix your pork, soy sauce, pepper, salt, flour, ginger, cloves and turmeric together. Make sure your pork is covered, and then let it marinate for an hour.
2. Press sauté, and add in your oil. Allow your oil to heat up before adding in your garlic and onion, and stir well. Cook for two minutes, and then transfer to a bowl.
3. Add in your pork cubes, and brown for five minutes before putting them to the side.
4. Return your onion and garlic to your instant pot, adding in your cinnamon, pineapple, stock, dates, and bay leaf. Stir well. Cover, and cook on high pressure for thirty-five minutes.
5. Set your pot to simmer, and add in your Swiss chard, cooking for one to two minutes. Discard the bay leaf, and then divide your mixture into bowls, serving warm.

Salmon with Vegetables

Serves: 2

Time: 15 Minutes

Ingredients:

- 2 Salmon Fillets, Boneless
- ½ Teaspoon Sweet Paprika
- ½ Teaspoon Cumin
- 1 Carrot, Chopped
- 1 Celery Stalk, Chopped
- 1 Yellow Onion, Chopped
- 1 Cup Broccoli Florets, Chopped Rough
- 2 Tablespoons Dry Sherry
- Sea Salt & Black Pepper to Taste
- 1 Cup Water

Directions:

1. Get out a heatproof pan, and add your onion, broccoli, carrot and celery in it. Season with salt and pepper, making sure it's covered.
2. Put your salmon fillets on top, seasoning them with paprika, cumin, and salt and pepper. Add in your dry sherry.
3. Add your water into your instant pot, and then place in your trivet. Put your pan on the trivet, and cook on high pressure for five minutes. Use a quick release, and then serve warm.

Tikka Masala

Serves: 2

Time: 35 Minutes

Ingredients:

- ½ Tablespoon Olive Oil
- ½ Tablespoon Butter
- ½ lb. Chicken Breasts, Skinless & Boneless
- 1 Yellow Onion, Small & Chopped
- Sea Salt & Black Pepper to Taste
- ½ Teaspoon Coriander
- ½ Tablespoon Garam Masala
- ½ Teaspoon Turmeric
- ½ Teaspoon Chili Powder
- 3 Cloves Garlic, Minced
- 1 Inch Ginger Piece, Peeled & Grated
- 1 ½ Tablespoons yogurt
- 7 Ounces Canned Tomatoes, Crushed
- 1 Tablespoon Almond Butter

Directions:

1. Add your oil and butter to your instant pot, and then press sauté. Allow it to heat up before adding in your own. Stir and cook for about five minutes.
2. Add in your salt, pepper, Garam masala, chili powder, turmeric, coriander, ginger, tomatoes and garlic. Stir, and cook for a minute more.
3. Add in your chicken breasts, cooking for sixteen minutes on manual.
4. Transfer it to a cutting board, shredding and setting it to the side.
5. Blend the mix from the pot using an immersion blender, adding in your almond butter and yogurt. Stir gently.
6. Add your chicken back in, and stir again before serving.

Lemon & Olive Chicken

Serves: 2

Time: 28 Minutes

Ingredients:

- Pinch Cumin
- 2 Chicken Breasts, Skinless & Boneless
- Sea Salt & Black Pepper to Taste
- 3 Tablespoons Butter
- ½ Lemon, Juiced
- 2 Lemon Slices
- ½ Cup Chicken Stock
- ½ Cup Green Olives, Pitted
- 3 Tablespoons Red Onion, Chopped

Directions:

1. Press sauté on your instant pot, adding in your chicken breasts. Season with cumin, salt and pepper. Brown for three minutes per side.
2. Add in your lemon juice, lemon slices, stock, butter, onion, and olives. Stir before cooking on high pressure for ten minutes.
3. Serve warm.

Salmon with Pesto Pasta

Serves: 2

Time: 20 Minutes

Ingredients:

- 2 Cups Water
- 8 Ounces Pasta
- 6 Ounces Smoked Salmon, Flaked
- Sea Salt & Black Pepper to Taste
- ½ Teaspoon Lemon Juice, Fresh
- ½ Teaspoon Lemon Zest, Grated
- 2 Tablespoons Butter

Pesto:

- 2 Tablespoons Walnuts
- 1 Clove Garlic
- 5 Cups Spinach Leaves
- 2 Tablespoons Olive Oil
- 1 Tablespoon Lemon Zest, Grated
- ½ Cup Parmesan, Grated
- ½ Cup Heavy Cream

Directions:

1. Get out a food processor and pulse your walnuts, spina, garlic, olive oil, a tablespoon of lemon zest, a half a cup of heavy cream, and parmesan together. Put it to the side.
2. Place your pasta into the instant pot, and add in your butter and water. Cover, cooking on high pressure for four minutes. Use a quick release.
3. Drain your pasta, and then clean out your instant pot.
4. Press sauté, and then add in your salmon. Season with salt, pepper, a half a teaspoon of lemon zest, lemon juice and pasta. Cook for two minutes.
5. Add in your pesto, making sure it's mixed.

Chicken & Dates

Serves: 2

Time: 40 Minutes

Ingredients:

- 4 Chicken Thighs, Skinless & Boneless
- Sea Salt & Black Pepper to Taste
- 1 Teaspoon Cumin
- ½ Tablespoon Olive Oil
- 1 Teaspoon Smoked Paprika
- 1 Teaspoon Coriander
- 1 Clove Garlic, Minced
- ½ Yellow Onion, Chopped
- 1 Carrot, Chopped
- 14 Ounces Tomatoes, Chopped
- 4 Medjol Dates, Chopped
- 4 Tablespoons Chicken Stock
- ½ Lemon, Cut into Wedges
- 4 Tablespoon Green Olives, Pitted
- 2 Tablespoon Pine Nuts
- Mint, Chopped for Garnish

Directions:

1. Mix your chicken thighs with your salt, pepper, oil, paprika, coriander and cumin.
2. Press sauté on your instant pot, adding in your chicken. Brown for five minutes per side.
3. Add in your onion, carrot, tomatoes, garlic, stock, olives, and dates. Stir well, and cook on high pressure for twenty minutes.
4. Sprinkle with pine nuts and mints before serving.

Lamb Chops

Serves: 2
Time: 38 Minutes
Ingredients:

- 1 Onion, Small & Sliced
- 1 Tablespoon Butter
- 2 Lamb Loin Chops, 4 Ounces Each
- 1 Clove Garlic, Crushed
- 14 Ounces Diced Tomatoes, Canned & Sugar Free
- 1 Cup Chicken Broth
- 1 Cup Carrot, Peeled & Sliced
- 1 Teaspoon Rosemary
- 2 Tablespoons Cornstarch
- 1 Tablespoon Water, Cold
- Sea Salt & Black Pepper to Taste

Directions:

1. Press sauté on your instant pot, adding in your butter. Once the butter is heated, add in your lamb chops. Sear for two to three minutes per side. They should be browned, and then take them out and set them to the side.
2. Place your garlic and onion into your instant pot, cooking for two to three minutes. Press cancel, and then add in your cooked lamb chops and all of your remaining ingredients.
3. Cook on high pressure for ten minutes. Use a quick release.
4. In a small bowl, dissolve your cornstarch and water to create a slurry.
5. Press sauté on your instant pot, adding in your cornstarch mixture. Stir and cook for one to two minutes.
6. Serve warm.

Spicy Salmon

Serves: 2

Time: 15 Minutes

Ingredients:

- 2 Salmon Fillets, Boneless
- ½ Lemon, Juiced
- ½ Lemon, Sliced
- 1 Tablespoon Chili Pepper, Minced
- 1 Cup Water
- Sea Salt & Black Pepper to Taste

Directions:

1. Mix your salmon, chili pepper, lemon juice, salt and pepper. Make sure your salmon is well coated.
2. Put your water in your instant pot before adding your steamer basket. Put your fish inside, and then cover with lemon slices. Cook on high pressure for five minutes.
3. Serve warm.

Beef Curry

Serves: 2

Time: 2 Hours 5 Minutes

Ingredients:

Marinade:

- 1 Tablespoon Coconut Oil
- ½ Teaspoon Ginger
- ½ Teaspoon Turmeric
- ½ Teaspoon Garlic
- Sea Salt & Black Pepper to Taste

Curry:

- 1 ½ Teaspoon Coconut Oil
- 1 lb. Beef Roast, Cubed
- 1 Onion, Small & Chopped
- ½ Cup Coconut Milk
- ½ Cinnamon Stick
- 1 Small Plantain, Peeled & Chunked
- 2 Kaffir Lime Leaves
- ½ Tablespoon Coriander, Chopped

Directions:

1. Mix your beef with a tablespoon of oil, seasoning with your turmeric, garlic, ginger, salt and pepper. Allow it to marinate for an hour.
2. Press sauté, and add one and a half teaspoons of oil, letting it heat up. Add in your beef, and stir. Brown for five minutes per side.
3. Add in your onion, lime leaves, coconut milk and cinnamon. Stir, cooking for thirty-five minutes on manual. Use a quick release.
4. Press sauté, and then add in your plantain, and allow it to simmer for three to four more minutes.
5. Sprinkle with coriander before serving.

Mediterranean Cod

Serves: 2

Time: 25 Minutes

Ingredients:

- 1 Yellow Onion, Small & Chopped
- 2 Cod Fillets, Boneless
- 1 ½ Tablespoons Butter
- 1/3 Lemon, Juiced
- Sea Salt & Black Pepper to Taste
- ½ Teaspoon Oregano
- 12 Ounces Tomatoes, Canned & Chopped

Directions:

1. Press sauté and add in your butter. Let it melt.
2. Add your salt, pepper, onion, tomatoes, oregano and lemon juice. Stir well, and cook for ten minutes.
3. Add your fish, and then cook on high pressure for five minutes. Use a quick release.

Cod in Orange Sauce

Serves: 2

Time: 20 Minutes

Ingredients:

- A Drizzle of Olive Oil
- 2 Cod Fillets, Boneless
- ½ Orange, Zested & Juiced
- 1 Inch Ginger, Grated
- 2 Sprigs Onions, Chopped
- ½ Cup Fish Stock
- Sea Salt & Black Pepper to Taste

Directions:

1. Season your cod with salt and pepper, drizzling it with oil.
2. Mix your orange juice, orange zest, stock, ginger, and sprigs of onion into your instant pot. Stir well.
3. Add in a steamer basket, putting your fish on the steamer basket.
4. Cook on high pressure for seven minutes, and then use a quick release.
5. Serve drizzled with your orange sauce.

Cheesy Honey Pork Roast

Serves: 2

Time: 40 Minutes

Ingredients:

- 1 lb. Pork Roast
- 1 Tablespoon Soy Sauce
- 2 Tablespoons Parmesan Cheese, Grated
- 2 Tablespoon Honey, Raw
- ½ Tablespoon Basil
- ½ Tablespoon Garlic, Minced
- ½ Tablespoon Olive Oil
- ½ Tablespoon Cornstarch
- ½ Cup Water
- Sea Salt to Taste

Directions:

1. Place all of your ingredients into the instant pot, stirring well.
2. Press the meat/stew button, and then set your time to thirty-five minutes.
3. Use a natural pressure release and serve warm.

Beef & Artichokes

Serves: 2

Time: 25 Minutes

Ingredients:

- ½ Tablespoon Olive Oil
- 1 lb. Beef, Ground
- 1 Yellow Onion Chopped
- ½ Teaspoon Garlic
- ½ Teaspoon Oregano
- ½ Teaspoon Dill
- ½ Teaspoon Onion
- Sea Salt & Black Pepper to Taste
- 10 Ounces Artichoke Hearts, Frozen
- 1/3 Cup Water
- ½ Teaspoon Apple Cider Vinegar
- 3 Tablespoons Avocado Mayonnaise

Directions:

1. Add in your oil, and press sauté. Allow it to heat up, and add in your onion. Cook and stir for five minutes.
2. Throw in your beef, seasoning with onion, garlic, dill, oregano, salt and pepper. Stir, cooking for another three minutes.
3. Add in your artichokes and water, stirring well. Cook on manual for seven minutes before using a quick release.
4. Drain any excess water, adding in your vinegar and mayonnaise. Stir well, and serve warm.

Fish Curry

Serves: 2

Time: 30 Minutes

Ingredients:

- 1 Onion, Chopped
- 1 Tablespoon Olive Oil
- 1 Teaspoon Ginger, Fresh & Grated Fine
- 2 Cloves Garlic, Minced
- 1 Teaspoon Cumin
- 1 Tablespoon Curry Powder
- 1 Teaspoon Coriander
- ½ Teaspoon Red Chili Powder
- ¼ Teaspoon Turmeric
- 1 Cup Coconut Milk, Unsweetened
- ¾ lb. Fish Fillets, Chopped
- ½ Cup Tomatoes, Chopped
- 1 Serrano Pepper, Seeded & Chopped
- ½ Tablespoon Lemon Juice, Fresh

Directions:

1. Press sauté, and then add in your garlic, ginger and onion. Cook for four to five minutes, and then add in your spices. Cook for another minute.
2. Add your coconut milk in, and mix well.
3. Press cancel, and add in your tomatoes, fish, and Serrano pepper. Stir well.
4. Cook on low pressure for five minutes, and allow for a natural pressure release.
5. Stir in your lemon juice before serving warm.

Shrimp Fried Rice

Serves: 2

Time: 45 Minutes

Ingredients:

- 1 Egg
- 1 Tablespoon Sesame Oil
- 1 Clove Garlic, Minced
- ½ Red Onion, Chopped
- ½ Cup Peas
- ½ Cup Shrimp, Frozen, Washed & Tailed
- ½ Cup Carrots
- ½ Tablespoon Soy Sauce
- 1 Cup Water
- ½ Cup Brown Rice
- 1 Teaspoon Apple Cider Vinegar
- ¼ Teaspoon Cayenne Pepper
- ½ Teaspoon Ginger, Minced
- ¼ Teaspoon Sea Salt, Fine

Directions:

1. Press sauté on your instant pot, and allow it to heat for two minutes before adding in your sesame oil.
2. Throw in your garlic and onion, cooking until your onion turns slightly brown.
3. Add in your peas and carrots, cooking for another four to five minutes.
4. Add in your minced ginger, soy sauce, shrimp, water, vinegar, salt and pepper. Allow it to simmer for three to four minutes.
5. Rinse your brown rice with water, adding it into the pot before cracking an egg into the mixture. Make sure to stir well.
6. Cook on high pressure for twenty-two minutes.
7. Use a natural pressure release for ten minutes before using a quick release to get rid of any remaining pressure.
8. Serve warm.

Cajun Chicken Fried Rice

Serves: 2

Time: 25 Minutes

Ingredients:

- ½ Tablespoon Cajun Seasoning
- ½ lb. Chicken Breast, Cubed
- ½ Tablespoon Olive Oil
- ½ Onion, Diced
- 1 Clove Garlic, Minced
- ½ Tablespoon Tomato Paste
- ¾ Cup White Rice, Rinsed
- 1 Cup Vegetable Broth
- 1 Red Bell Pepper, Diced

Directions:

1. Put your oil in your instant pot and press sauté. Add in your onion and garlic, cooking until your garlic browns. You'll need to stir frequently.
2. Press cancel, and then add in your rice, Cajun seasoning, chicken breast, tomato paste, bell pepper and vegetable broth. Stir until well combined.
3. Cook on high pressure for ten minutes.
4. Use a natural pressure release for ten minutes, and then use a quick release to get rid of any remaining pressure.
5. Stir well before serving.

Buttered Chicken

Serves: 2

Time: 22 Minutes

Ingredients:

- 2 Chicken Thighs, Boneless, Skinless & Cubed
- ½ Cup Heavy Cream
- 2 Tablespoons Butter
- 1 Tablespoon Onion, Minced
- ½ Tablespoon Garlic, Minced
- ½ Tablespoon Ginger, Minced
- ½ Teaspoon Chili Powder
- ½ Teaspoon Cumin
- ½ Cup Water
- ¼ Teaspoon Sea Salt, Fine

Directions:

1. Put your butter in the instant pot, and then press sauté. Add in your onion and chicken, cooking until your chicken is slightly browned.
2. Add all of your remaining ingredients, and mix well.
3. Cook on high pressure for eight minutes.
4. Use a quick release, and serve warm.

Glazed Salmon

Serves: 2

Time: 20 Minutes

Ingredients:

- 2 Salmon Fillets, 5 Ounces Each
- Sea Salt & Black Pepper to Taste
- 1 Jalapeno Pepper, Seeded & Chopped Fine
- 2 Cloves Garlic, Minced
- 1 Tablespoon Parsley, Fresh & Chopped
- 2 Tablespoons Lime Juice, Fresh
- 1 Tablespoon Honey, Raw
- 1 Tablespoon Olive Oil
- 1 Tablespoon Hot Water
- ½ Teaspoon Paprika
- ½ Teaspoon Cumin

Directions:

1. Sprinkle your sea salt and black pepper over your salmon fillets
2. Get out a bowl and add all remaining ingredients together, mixing well.
3. Place a cup of water into your instant pot before adding in your trivet.
4. Place your fillets in your trivet, and press steam. Cook for five minutes before using a quick release.
5. Serve drizzled with sauce.

Crispy Chicken

Serves: 2

Time: 35 Minutes

Ingredients:

- 1 lb. Chicken Breasts, Skinless Boneless
- ½ Teaspoon Chili Powder
- ½ Teaspoon Oregano
- ½ Tablespoon Cumin
- Sea Salt & Black Pepper to Taste
- ½ Orange, Zested & Juiced
- 2 Cloves Garlic, Minced
- 1 Yellow Onion, Small & Chopped
- 1 Tablespoon Adobo Sauce
- 1 Tablespoon Olive Oil
- 2 Tablespoons Cilantro, Fresh & Chopped

Sauce:

- 1 Chipotle Pepper
- 3 Tablespoons Mayonnaise
- ½ Tablespoon Milk
- Sea Salt for Serving
- Garlic Powder for Serving
- 2 Tortillas for Serving

Directions:

1. Mix your cumin, chili powder, oregano, salt, pepper and chicken breasts together. Toss until it's well coated.
2. Set your instant pot to sauté, and then add in your oil. Heat it up, and then brown your chicken breasts for one minute per side. Transfer your chicken to a plate.
3. Add in your onion and garlic, cooking for two minutes. Remember to stir well so it doesn't burn.
4. Return your chicken to your instant pot, adding in your orange zest, orange juice, stock, bay leaf, cilantro, and adobo sauce. Stir well, and cook on high pressure for ten minutes.
5. Transfer your chicken breasts to a cutting board, allowing it to cool enough to shred.
6. Transfer your shredded chicken to a bowl, drizzling with some of your cooking liquid. Toss until well coated.
7. Spread your chicken on a lined baking sheet, and preheat your broiler. Broil for ten minutes.
8. In your blender, blend your mayonnaise, chipotle pepper, milk, and salt and garlic powder. Pulse until well combined.
9. Divide your chicken on tortillas and then add your sauce. Roll to serve.

Turkey Meatballs

Serves: 2
Time: 35 Minutes
Ingredients:
Sauce:

- ¼ Cup Soy Sauce
- 2 Tablespoons Rice Vinegar
- 1 Teaspoon Ginger, Fresh & Grated
- 1 Tablespoon Canola Oil
- 1 Clove Garlic, Minced
- 1 ½ Tablespoons Brown Sugar
- ½ Tablespoon Cornstarch
- ½ Cup Water
- ¼ Teaspoon Black Pepper

Meatballs:

- ½ lb. Ground Turkey
- 2 Saltine Crackers, Crushed
- 1 ½ Tablespoons Buttermilk
- 2 Tablespoon Scallions, Sliced
- ½ Teaspoon Garlic Powder
- ½ Tablespoon Canola Oil
- Sea Salt & Black Pepper to Taste

Directions:

1. Mix all of your sauce ingredients into a bowl, making sur they're well combined.
2. Mix all of your meatball ingredients in a bowl except for your oil, and mix well. It should be well combined.
3. Make equal sized meatballs, and then put your oil into your instant pot. Press sauté, and add your meatballs in. cook for four to five minutes. Your meatballs should be browned on all sides.
4. Press cancel, and then pour your sauce over your meatballs.
5. Cook on high pressure for ten minutes.
6. Use a natural pressure release, and serve warm.

Mediterranean Calamari

Serves: 2

Time: 15 Minutes

Ingredients:

- 1 lb. Calamari, Chopped
- ½ Red Onion, Sliced
- 1 Tablespoon Olive Oil
- ½ Cup Red Wine
- 1 Clove Garlic, Chopped
- 1 Celery Stalk, Chopped
- 1 Cup Tomatoes, Crushed
- 2 Tablespoons Italian Parsley, Chopped
- 1 Sprig Rosemary, Fresh
- Sea Salt & Black Pepper to Taste

Directions:

1. Season your olive oil with salt and pepper, and toss your calamari pieces in it.
2. Add your wine, tomatoes, rosemary, garlic, red onion and celery into your instant pot.
3. Put your calamari in a steamer basket, placing it right over the liquid.
4. Cook on high pressure for four minutes.
5. Use a quick release, and sprinkle with parsley before serving.

Simple Pho

Serves: 2

Time: 50 Minutes

Ingredients:

- 1 lb. Chicken Pieces, Bone In & Skin On
- 1 Small Piece Ginger, Grated
- 1 Onion, Small & Quartered
- ½ Tablespoons Coriander Seeds, Toasted
- ½ Teaspoon Cardamom Pods
- 2 Cloves
- ½ Lemongrass Stalk, Chopped
- ½ Cinnamon Stick
- 2 Tablespoons Fish Sauce
- ½ Bok Choy, Chopped
- ½ Daikon Root, Spiralized
- 1 Tablespoon Green Onions, Chopped

Directions:

1. Mix your ginger, chicken, onion, coriander seeds, cardamom, cloves, lemongrass, fish sauce, daikon, bok choy and water together. Stir well, and cook on high pressure for thirty minutes.
2. Strain your soup, and shred your chicken.
3. Serve with green onions.

Sweet Short Ribs

Serves: 2

Time: 1 Hour 10 Minutes

Ingredients:

- ½ Tablespoon Olive Oil
- 1 Teaspoon Black Pepper
- ¾ Tablespoons Garlic, Chopped
- 2 Short Ribs, Trimmed
- 1 Tablespoons Scallions, Sliced Thin
- ½ Tablespoon Soy Sauce
- ½ Cup Water
- ¼ Cup Barbecue Sauce
- ¾ Tablespoon Brown Sugar
- ¾ Tablespoon Vinegar
- ¾ Tablespoons Red Chili Paste
- 1 Tablespoon Cold Water
- ½ Tablespoon Cornstarch

Directions:

1. Press sauté on your instant pot, and then add in your oil. Once your oil is hot, add in your short ribs. Cook for five minutes. They should be brown.
2. Put your short ribs on a plate.
3. Place your scallions and garlic into your instant pot, cooking for a minute. Make sure to stir constantly.
4. Add in your pepper, vinegar, water, barbecue sauce, sugar, red chili paste and soy sauce. Stir until well combined.
5. Close the lid, cooking on high pressure for forty-five minutes.
6. Use a quick release, and then remove your ribs. Put them to the side.
7. Press sauté, and allow your sauce to simmer.
8. Whisk cold water and cornstarch together in a bowl, adding it to your sauce. Cook for two more minutes. It should thicken.
9. Serve your sauce over your ribs, and garnish with scallions.

Steamed Mussels

Serves: 2

Time: 15 Minutes

Ingredients:

- ½ Tablespoon Pepper
- ½ Cup White Wine
- ½ Tablespoon Parsley
- Sea Salt to Taste
- 1 Cup Tomatoes, Diced
- 2 lbs. Fresh Mussels, Cleaned & Rinsed

Directions:

1. Add your wine and tomatoes into your instant pot, and then season with salt, pepper and parsley.
2. Add in a steamer basket, lowered to the liquid, and then place your mussels in the steamer basket.
3. Cook on high pressure for three minutes before using a quick release.
4. Serve with the tomato and wine sauce.

Picadillo

Serves: 2

Time: 25 Minutes

Ingredients:

- 1 Clove Garlic, Minced
- 1 Tomato, Chopped
- ½ Onion, Large & Chopped
- ¾ lb. Ground Beef
- ½ Teaspoon Sea Salt, Fine
- 1 Bay Leaf
- 1 Tablespoon Olives, pitted
- 2 Ounces Tomato Sauce
- ½ Tablespoon Cilantro, Fresh & Chopped
- ½ Cup Water

Directions:

1. Press sauté, and then add your beef, breaking your meat up as it browns.
2. Add in the rest of your ingredients before mixing well.
3. Cook on high pressure for fifteen minutes, and then use a quick release. Serve with rice or with a side salad as desired.

Beef Bourguignon

Serves: 2

Time: 1 Hour

Ingredients:

- ½ lb. Beef Stew Meat
- 2 Bacon Slices
- 1 Clove Garlic, Minced
- 1 Onion, Chopped
- 2 Carrots, Chopped
- 1 Tablespoon Thyme
- 1 Tablespoon Parsley
- ½ Cup Beef Stock
- 1 Potato, Large & Cubed
- ½ Tablespoon Honey, Raw
- ½ Tablespoon Olive Oil
- ½ Cup Red Wine

Directions:

1. Place your oil in the instant pot, and then press sauté. Add in your beef, cooking for four minutes. Your beef should be browned, and then you can place it to the side.
2. Add your bacon and onion in, cooking until your onion is translucent.
3. Add your beef back in along with the rest of your ingredients.
4. Cook on high pressure for a half hour, and then allow for a natural pressure release. Serve warm.

Chicken Curry

Serves: 2

Time: 55 Minutes

Ingredients:

- 1 Bay Leaf
- Small Piece Cinnamon Stick
- 1 Tablespoon Butter
- 1 Cup Onion, Chopped
- Pinch Cumin Seeds
- ½ Tablespoon Garlic, Minced
- ½ Tablespoon Ginger, Grated
- 1 Tablespoon Tomato Paste
- Pinch Turmeric Powder
- 1 Tablespoon Coriander Seeds
- Pinch Cayenne Pepper
- 1 lb. Chicken Thighs
- 1 Cup Potato, Cubed
- Sea Salt & Black Pepper to Taste
- ¼ Cup Water
- 1 Teaspoon Garam Masala
- 1 Tablespoon Cashew Paste
- 2 Tablespoons Cilantro, Fresh & Chopped

Directions:

1. Press sauté on your instant pot, and then add in your butter. Allow it to melt, and then add in your cinnamon, bay leaf and cumin. Stir well.
2. Add in your onion, garlic and ginger sauté for six minutes.
3. Add in your tomato paste, stirring and cooking for another three minutes.
4. Add turmeric, cayenne, coriander, salt, chicken, pepper and water into your instant pot. Cook on high pressure for fifteen minutes.
5. Add in your potatoes and Garam masala. Cook on manual pressure for six minutes. Use a quick release.
6. Add in your cilantro and cashew paste, stirring well.

Taco Chicken

Serves: 2

Time: 35 Minutes

Ingredients:

- ½ Tablespoon Olive Oil
- ½ Onion, Small & Chopped
- ½ Teaspoon Red Chili Powder
- 1 Clove Garlic, Minced
- ½ lb. Chicken Thighs, Boneless, Skinless & Cut into 1 Inch Chunks
- 8 Ounces Black Beans, Canned, Drained & Rinsed
- ½ Cup Salsa
- 1/3 Cup Long Grain White Rice
- 2 Tablespoons Cheddar Cheese, Grated
- 1 Cup Chicken Broth
- 2 Tablespoons Cilantro, Fresh & Chopped

Directions:

1. Put your oil in your instant pot, and press sauté. Add in your onion, allowing it to cook for two minutes.
2. Add in your chili powder and garlic, cooking for one more minute. Press cancel, and stir in your beans, salsa, rice, broth and chicken.
3. Cook on high pressure for ten minutes.
4. Use a quick release, and top with cheese and cilantro before serving.

Beef Stew

Serves: 2

Time: 35 Minutes

Ingredients:

- 1 lb. Beef Meat, Cubed
- 1 Tablespoon Flour
- 1 Tablespoon Olive Oil
- 1 Yellow Onion, Chopped
- Sea Salt & Black Pepper to Taste
- 1 Clove Garlic, Minced
- 3 Tablespoon Red Wine
- 1 Celery Stalk, Chopped
- 2 Carrots, Chopped
- ½ lb. Red Potatoes, Chopped
- ½ Tablespoons Tomato Paste
- 2 Tablespoons Parsley, Chopped
- 1 Cup Beef Stock

Directions:

1. Mix your beef, salt, pepper and four together in a bowl. Toss until coated.
2. Press sauté on your instant pot, adding in your oil.
3. Once oil begins to shier, add in your beef. Brown your beef on all sides before transferring it to a bowl.
4. Set it to the side, and add in your wine to your instant pot, pressing sauté. Cook for a few minutes.
5. Return your beef to your instant pot. Add in your garlic, onions, potatoes, carrots, celery, tomato paste and stock. Stir well, and cook on high pressure for twenty minutes.
6. Use a quick release, and add in your parsley. Serve warm.

Side Dish Recipes

These side dishes are perfect for two people. Just pick a meat and pair it with any of these delicious recipes to complete your dinner.

Sesame Carrots

Serves: 2

Time: 15 Minutes

Ingredients:

- 1 Scallion, Chopped
- 2 Teaspoons Toasted Sesame Seeds
- 1 Teaspoons Ginger, Fresh & Grated
- 1 Carrot, Chunked
- 1 ½ Teaspoons Rice Vinegar
- 2 Teaspoons Sesame Oil
- 1 ½ Teaspoons Soy Sauce
- Sea Salt & Black Pepper to Taste

Directions:

1. Place all of your ingredients except for your sesame into your instant pot, and press steam. Cook for ten minutes.
2. If any liquid is still in your instant pot, simmer until dry.
3. Add in your sesame seeds and stir well before serving.

Stir Fried Broccoli

Serves: 2

Time: 10 Minutes

Ingredients:

- 1 Inch Piece Ginger, Peeled & Sliced
- 1 Head Broccoli, Chopped into Florets
- 1 Tablespoon Peanut Oil
- 1 Clove Garlic, Crushed
- ¼ Cup Water
- 1 Tablespoon Soy Sauce
- Sea Salt & Black Pepper to Taste

Directions:

1. Press sauté and add in your oil.
2. Place your ginger and garlic into your instant pot, sautéing until golden brown.
3. Toss in your broccoli, and sauté until it turns a bright green.
4. Add the rest of your ingredients into your instant pot, stirring well.
5. Press manual, and cook for two minutes.
6. Use a quick release before serving warm.

Butter Rice

Serves: 2

Time: 30 Minutes

Ingredients:

- ¾ Cup French Onion Soup
- ¾ Cup Stock
- ¼ Cup Butter
- 1 Cup Brown Rice
- Sea Salt to Taste

Directions:

1. Toss all of your ingredients into your instant pot, and then press manual. Cook for twenty-two minutes, and then allow for a natural pressure release for two minutes.
2. Use a quick release for the remaining pressure.
3. Fluff before serving.

Potato Wedges

Serves: 2
Time: 20 Minutes
Ingredients:

- 1 Cup Water
- Sea Salt & Black Pepper to Taste
- Pinch Baking Soda
- 1 Teaspoon Onion Powder
- ½ Teaspoon Garlic Powder
- ¼ Teaspoon Cayenne Pepper
- ½ Teaspoon Oregano
- 2 Potatoes, Large & Cut into Medium Wedges
- 3 Quarts Sunflower Oil + 2 Tablespoons
- 1 Cup Flour
- ½ Cup Buttermilk
- 3 Tablespoons Cornstarch

Directions:

1. Place your water into your instant pot, adding in your baking soda and salt. Stir before adding in your steamer basket.
2. Get out a bowl and mix in your garlic, onion, salt, pepper, cayenne and oregano. Stir until combined.
3. Add in your potatoes, tossing until they're well coated, and then place them in your steamer basket.
4. Cook on high pressure for two minutes, and then mix your cornstarch and flour in a bowl.
5. In another bowl mix your buttermilk and a pinch of baking soda. Whisk well.
6. Drain your potatoes wedges and then dredge them through your flour mix.
7. Heat up a pan with your three quarts of oil over medium high heat, and then cook for four minutes.
8. Drain on a paper towel before serving.

Steamed Leeks

Serves: 2

Time: 20 Minutes

Ingredients:

- 2 Leeks, Trimmed & Halved Lengthwise
- 1/3 Cup Water
- ½ Tablespoon Butter
- Sea Salt & Black Pepper to Taste

Directions:

1. Place your water into your instant pot before lowering in your steamer basket. Place your leeks in the basket, seasoning with salt and pepper.
2. Cook on high pressure for five minutes. Use a quick release.
3. Clean your instant pot, putting your leeks on a plate.
4. Press sauté and then melt your butter before adding in your leeks again. Stir well, cooking for two to three more minutes. Serve warm.

Stir Fried Okra

Serves: 2

Time: 20 Minutes

Ingredients:

- 1 Onion, Chopped
- 1 lb. Okra, Chopped
- 1 Tablespoon Olive Oil
- 1 Tomato, Chopped
- 2 Cloves Garlic, Minced
- ¼ Teaspoon Turmeric
- ½ Teaspoon Cumin
- 1 Teaspoon Coriander
- ¼ Teaspoon Cayenne Pepper
- 1 Teaspoon Lemon Juice
- Sea Salt & Black Pepper to Taste

Directions:

1. Press sauté, adding in your oil.
2. Once your oil begins to shimmer, add in your cumin and garlic. Stir, cooking for a minute.
3. Add in your onion, stirring well and cooking for another two minutes.
4. Throw in the rest of your ingredients, and then stir well.
5. Cook on low pressure for five minutes, and serve warm.

Spicy Collard Greens

Serves: 2

Time: 40 Minutes

Ingredients:

- 2 Cups Chicken Stock
- 1 Bunch Collard Greens, Cut into Strips
- 1 Clove Garlic, Minced
- 2 Bacon Slices, Chopped
- 2 Teaspoons Creole Seasoning
- 1 Jalapeno, Chopped
- Splash Apple Cider Vinegar

Directions:

1. Press sauté and add in your bacon. Cook for four minutes before tossing in your garlic. Cook for a minute more, making sure to stir.
2. Add in your remaining ingredients and stir well.
3. Cook on high pressure for twenty-five minutes.
4. Use a quick release and serve warm.

Edamame & Rice

Serves: 2

Time: 25 Minutes

Ingredients:

- 1 Yellow Onion, Chopped
- ½ Tablespoon Olive Oil
- ½ Tablespoon Butter
- 1 Cup White Rice
- 2 Cups Chicken Stock
- Sea Salt & Black Pepper to Taste
- 3 Tablespoons White Wine
- ½ Cup Edamame
- S

Directions:

1. Press sauté, adding in your butter and oil.
2. Add in your onion, cooking for three minutes. Make sure to stir well.
3. Add in your rice, stirring well and cooking for another two minutes.
4. Add in your remaining ingredients, and cook on high pressure for seven minutes. Use a quick release, and fluff before serving.

Fennel & Shallots

Serves: 2

Time: 20 Minutes

Ingredients:

- 1 Fennel Bulb, Large & Sliced
- Sea Salt & Black Pepper to Taste
- ½ lb. Shallots, Sliced
- ½ Cup Orange Juice
- 2 Tablespoons Olive Oil
- 1 Teaspoon Parsley, Chopped
- ½ Teaspoon Orange Zest, Grated

Directions:

1. Press sauté and heat up your oil.
2. Add in your shallots, and stir well. Cook for four minutes.
3. Add in your remaining ingredients, and cook on high pressure for seen minutes.
4. Use a quick release, and then serve warm.

Coconut Cabbage

Serves: 2

Time: 20 Minutes

Ingredients:

- ½ Brown Onion, Chopped
- ½ Tablespoon Coconut Oil
- Sea Salt & Black Pepper to Taste
- 1 Clove Garlic, Minced
- ½ Tablespoon Mustard Seeds
- ½ Chili Pepper, Chopped
- ½ Tablespoon Curry Powder
- ½ Tablespoon Turmeric Powder
- ½ Cabbage, Shredded
- ½ Carrot, Chopped
- 1 Tablespoon Lime Juice
- ½ Tablespoon Olive Oil
- 3 Tablespoons Water
- 4 Tablespoons Coconut, Desiccated

Directions:

1. Press sauté, adding in your coconut oil. Allow it to heat up, and then add in your onion, seasoning with salt and pepper. Cook for three minutes, and remember to stir so it doesn't stick
2. Adding all of your remaining ingredients, and stir well. Cook on high pressure for six minutes.
3. Use a quick release, and stir once more before serving.

Vegetable Medley

Serves: 2

Time: 20 Minutes

Ingredients:

- 1 Tablespoon Garlic, Crushed
- ½ Sweet Onion, Sliced
- 2 Tablespoons Olive Oil
- 1 Tablespoon Tomato Paste
- 1 Small Eggplant, Cubed
- 1 Green bell Pepper, Chunked
- 1 Red Bell Pepper, Chunked
- 1 Green Zucchini, Chopped
- ½ Yellow Squash, Peeled & Cubed
- 1 Teaspoon Italian Seasoning
- 6 Ounces Tomatoes, Canned & Chopped
- 1/3 Cup Vegetable Stock
- Sea Salt & Black Pepper to Taste

Directions:

1. Press sauté, adding in your oil. Allow your oil to heat up before throwing in your onions. Stir well, cooking for three minutes.
2. Add in your garlic and tomato paste, stirring well. Cook for a few more seconds.
3. Add in your zucchini, green bell pepper, red bell pepper, eggplant, squash, tomatoes, salt, pepper, and Italian seasoning. Add in your stock, and stir well. Cook on high pressure for seven minutes.
4. Use a quick release, and serve warm.

Squash Risotto

Serves: 2

Time: 25 Minutes

Ingredients:

- 1 Yellow Onion, Small & Chopped
- 1 Clove Garlic, Minced
- Drizzle Olive oil
- ½ Red Bell Pepper, Chopped
- 1 Cup Arborio Rice
- 1 Cup Butternut Squash, Chopped
- 1 ½ Cups Vegetable Stock
- 4 Ounces Mushrooms, Chopped
- 3 Tablespoons Dry White Wine
- Sea Salt & Black Pepper to Taste
- ¼ Teaspoon Oregano
- ¼ Teaspoon Coriander
- 1 ½ Cups Kale & Spinach Mix
- 1 Tablespoon Nutritional Yeast

Directions:

1. Press sauté, and then add in your oil. Place in your bell pepper, squash, onion and garlic. Cook for five minutes, stirring frequently.
2. Add in your stock, wine, salt, pepper, rice, mushrooms, coriander, and oregano. Stir, and then cook on high pressure for five minutes. Use a quick release.
3. Add in your spinach, kale, parsley and east. Stir, and allow it to sit for five minutes before serving.

Easy Cabbage

Serves: 2

Time: 20 Minutes

Ingredients:

- ½ lb. Turkey Sausage, Sliced
- ½ Cabbage, Shredded
- 2 Cloves Garlic, Minced
- 1 Teaspoon Sugar
- ½ Yellow Onion, Chopped
- 1 Teaspoon Balsamic Vinegar
- 1 Teaspoon Mustard
- Sea Salt & Black Pepper to Taste
- Drizzle of Olive Oil

Direction:

1. Push sauté, heating up your oil.
2. Add in your garlic, sausage and onion, cooking for five minutes.
3. Add in the remaining ingredients, and cook on high pressure for five minutes.
4. Use a quick release, and serve warm.

Broccoli Pasta

Serves: 2

Time: 15 Minutes

Ingredients:

- 2 Cups Water
- 8 Ounces Cheddar Cheese, Grated
- ½ lb. Pasta
- ½ Cup Half & Half
- ½ Cup Broccoli

Directions:

1. Place your pasta and water in the pot before adding in your steamer basket. Place your broccoli in the steamer basket.
2. Cook on high pressure for four minutes, and then drain the pasta. Transfer your pasta and broccoli into a clean pot.
3. Press sauté, and then add in your pasta, broccoli, cheese, and half and half. Stir well, cooking for two minutes.
4. Serve warm.

Chorizo & Beans

Serves: 2

Time: 55 Minutes

Ingredients:

- ½ lb. Black Beans
- 3 Ounces Chorizo, Chopped
- ½ Tablespoon Olive Oil
- ½ Yellow Onion, Chopped
- 3 Cloves Garlic, Minced
- ½ Orange
- 1 Bay Leaf
- 1 Quart Chicken Stock
- 1 Tablespoon Cilantro, Chopped
- Sea Salt & Black Pepper to Taste

Directions:

1. Press sauté before pouring your oil in your instant pot. Add in your chorizo, and cook for two minutes.
2. Add your onion, beans, orange, bay leaf, garlic, stock, salt and pepper. Cook on high pressure for forty minutes.
3. Discard the orange bay leaf. Add in your cilantro, and then serve warm.

Beet Salad

Serves: 2

Time: 40 Minutes

Ingredients:

Salad:

- 4 Medium Beets, Trimmed
- 2 Cups Baby Spinach, Fresh
- 1 Tablespoon Balsamic Vinegar
- 1 Tablespoon Feta Cheese, Crumbled

Dressing:

- 1 Tablespoon Olive Oil
- 1 Tablespoon Parsley, Fresh & Minced
- 2 Tablespoons Capers
- 1 Clove Garlic, Minced
- Sea Salt & Black Pepper to Taste

Directions:

1. Arrange your trivet in your instant pot after adding a cup of water into it. Put your beets on top of your trivet in a single layer.
2. Cook on high pressure for twenty minutes.
3. Use a quick release, and rinse the beets under cold water.
4. Slice them, adding them into a bowl.
5. Add in your spinach, drizzling with vinegar.
6. Add all dressing ingredients together in a bowl, stirring until well combined
7. Pour your dressing over your beet salad, stirring well before topping with cheese to serve.

Easy Spanish Rice

Serves: 2
Time: 25 Minutes
Ingredients:

- ½ Cup Rice
- ½ Tablespoon Butter
- ½ Tablespoon Olive Oil
- ½ Cup Tomato Sauce
- 1 Teaspoon Chili Powder
- ½ Cup Chicken Stock
- ½ Teaspoon Cumin
- ¼ Teaspoon Oregano
- 2 Tablespoons Tomatoes, Chopped
- Sea Salt & Black Pepper to Taste

Directions:

1. Add your oil into your instant pot, pressing sauté. Add in your rice, allowing it to cook for four minutes.
2. Add in your chili powder, cumin, tomato sauce, stock, oregano, tomatoes, salt and pepper. Stir well and cook on high pressure for eight minutes. Use a quick release.
3. Stir once more before serving.

Simple Spaghetti Sauce

Serves: 2

Time: 45

Ingredients:

- 1 Spaghetti Squash, Small
- 1 Cup Water
- ½ Cup Apple Juice
- 1 Tablespoon Duck Fat
- Sea Salt & Black Pepper to Taste

Directions:

1. Place your water into your instant pot before adding in your steamer basket. Add your squash in your steamer basket, and cook for thirty minutes on high pressure.
2. Use a quick release, and then halve your squash. Scoop the seeds out, and then clean your instant pot out. Press sauté, and add in your duck fat. Allow it to heat up.
3. Add your apple juice, salt and pepper in, letting it simmer for three minutes.
4. Divide between plates, and drizzle your sauce over your squash.

Cauliflower Rice

Serves: 2

Time: 25 Minutes

Ingredients:

- ½ Cauliflower Head, Florets Separated
- 1 Tablespoon Olive Oil
- Sea Salt & Black Pepper to Taste
- ¼ Teaspoon Parsley Flakes
- ¼ Teaspoon Cumin
- ¼ Teaspoon Paprika
- ¼ Teaspoon Turmeric
- 1 Cup Water
- 1/3 Lime, Juiced
- ½ Tablespoon Cilantro, Chopped

Directions:

1. Put water into your instant pot before adding in your steamer basket. Add in your cauliflower florets, and cook on high pressure for two minutes.
2. Discard the water, and then put your cauliflower on a plate.
3. Clean out your instant pot before adding in your oil. Press sauté and allow your oil to heat up.
4. Add your cauliflower and mash. Add in your pepper, salt, parsley, turmeric, paprika, cilantro and lime juice stir well and cook for ten minutes before serving.

Simple Artichokes

Serves: 2

Time: 30 Minutes

Ingredients:

- 2 Cups Artichokes, Trimmed & Tops Cut Off
- 1 Lemon, Cut into Wedges
- 1 Cup Water

Directions:

1. Rub the cuts on your artichokes down with lemon wedges.
2. Add in water, and then add in your steamer basket. Put your artichokes in, and then cook on high pressure for twenty minutes.
3. Serve warm.

Creamy Cabbage

Serves: 2

Time: 20 Minutes

Ingredients:

- 1 lb. Savory Cabbage, Chopped
- 1 Cup Beef Stock
- ½ Yellow Onion, Chopped
- ½ Cup Bacon, Chopped
- Pinch Nutmeg
- 1 Bay Leaf
- ½ Cup Coconut Milk
- 1 Tablespoon Parsley Flakes
- Sea Salt to Taste

Directions:

1. Press sauté, adding in your onion and bacon. Stir and cook for three minutes.
2. Add in your cabbage, bay leaf, and stock. Cook on manual for four minutes before using a quick release.
3. Press sauté, and then add in your nutmeg, salt and coconut milk. Discard your bay leaf, and then stir in your cabbage. Simmer for four minutes.
4. Sprinkle with parsley flakes and serve warm.

Sweet Brussel Sprouts

Serves: 2

Time: 15 Minutes

Ingredients:

- 1 Tablespoon Orange Juice
- ½ Teaspoon Orange Zest, Grated
- 2 Teaspoons Buttery Spread
- ½ lbs. Brussels Sprouts
- ½ Tablespoon Maple Syrup
- Sea Salt & Black Pepper to Taste

Directions:

1. Mix your buttery spread, orange juice, orange zest, Brussel sprouts, salt, pepper and Brussel sprouts together in your instant pot.
2. Cook on high pressure for four minutes.
3. Use a quick release and serve warm.

Garlic Mashed Potatoes

Serves: 2

Time: 10 Minutes

Ingredients:

- ½ Cup Vegetable Broth
- 3 Cloves Garlic, Minced
- 2 Russet Potatoes
- 2 Tablespoons Parsley, Chopped
- ¼ Cup Milk, Low Fat
- Sea Salt to Taste

Directions:

1. Cut your potatoes into chunks, placing your chunks into your instant pot. Add in your broth and garlic.
2. Cook on high pressure for five minutes, and then use a natural pressure release.
3. Mash your potatoes, adding in your parsley, milk and salt. Stir well, and serve hot.

Brussel Sprout Salad

Serves: 2

Time: 20 Minutes

Ingredients:

- ½ lb. Brussels Sprouts, Trimmed & Halved
- ½ Tablespoon Butter, Unsalted & Melted
- ½ Cup Pomegranate Seeds
- ¼ Cup Almonds, Chopped

Directions:

1. Add a cup of water into your instant pot, and then put your steamer basket in your instant pot.
2. Place your Brussel sprouts in your steamer basket, and cook on high pressure for four minutes.
3. Use a quick release
4. Place your Brussel sprouts on a serving plate, drizzling with melted butter.
5. Top with almonds and pomegranate seeds before serving.

Kale & Carrots

Serves: 2

Time: 25 Minutes

Ingredients:

- 1 Tablespoon Butter
- 10 Ounces Kale, Chopped Rough
- 3 Carrots, Sliced
- 4 Cloves Garlic, Minced
- 1 Yellow Onion, Chopped
- ½ Cup Chicken Stock
- A Splash Balsamic Vinegar
- Sea Salt & Black Pepper to Taste
- ¼ Teaspoon Red Pepper Flakes

Directions:

1. Pres sauté and melt your butter.
2. Add in your carrots and onions, cooking for three minutes.
3. Add in your garlic, and stir well. Cook for a minute.
4. Add in your stock and kale, cooking on high pressure for seven minutes.
5. Add in your vinegar and pepper flakes. Stir well and serve warm.

Cabbage & Beet Mix

Serves: 2

Time: 30 Minutes

Ingredients:

- 2 Cups Chicken Stock
- 1 Apple, Small, Cored & Chopped
- ½ Green Cabbage, Small & Chopped
- ½ Yellow Onion, Chopped
- 1 Beet, Chopped
- 1 Carrot, Chopped
- ½ Tablespoon Ginger, Grated
- ½ Teaspoon Gelatin
- 1 Tablespoon Parsley
- Sea Salt to Taste

Directions:

1. In your instant pot mix together all of your ingredients.
2. Cook on high pressure for twenty minutes before using a quick release. Serve warm.

Carrots & Cabbage

Serves: 2

Time: 30 Minutes

Ingredients:

- 1 Tablespoon Coconut Oil
- 1 Onion, Small & Sliced
- Sea Salt to Taste
- 1 Clove Garlic, Chopped
- ½ Jalapeno Pepper, Seeded & Chopped
- ½ Tablespoon Mild Curry Powder
- ½ Head Cabbage, Shredded
- 1 Carrot, Small, Peeled & Sliced
- 1 Tablespoon Lemon Juice, Fresh
- ¼ Cup Coconut, Unsweetened & Desiccated
- 1/3 Cup Water

Directions:

1. Put your coconut oil in the instant pot, pressing sauté. Add in your salt and onion, cooking for four more minutes.
2. Add in your jalapeno, curry powder and garlic, cooking for a minute more. Press cancel, and add in all of your remaining ingredients. Stir well.
3. Cook on high pressure for five minutes, and use a natural pressure release for five minutes. Use a quick release for any remaining pressure.

Garlic Broccoli

Serves: 2

Time: 25 Minutes

Ingredients:

- 1 Tablespoon Olive Oil
- 1 Broccoli Head, Florets
- 5 Cloves Garlic, Minced
- ½ Cup Water
- 1 Tablespoon Olive Oil
- 1 Tablespoon Rice Wine
- Sea Salt & Black Pepper to Taste

Directions:

1. Place your water in your instant pot before adding in your steamer basket. Put your broccoli in your steamer basket, and cook on high pressure for ten minutes.
2. Transfer your broccoli to an ice water, cooling it down. Drain and then transfer it to a bowl.
3. Clean your instant pot, and then press sauté. Let your oil heat up, and then add in your garlic.
4. Stir and cook for one to two minutes.
5. Add in your salt, pepper and wine. Stir well, and cook for a minute more.
6. Add your broccoli back in, and stir well. Cook for one to two minutes more before serving warm.

Spinach & Tomatoes

Serves: 2

Time: 20 Minutes

Ingredients:

- 1 Teaspoon Garlic, Minced
- 1 Onion, Small & Chopped
- 1 Tablespoon Olive Oil
- 5 Cups Spinach, Fresh & Chopped
- ½ Cup Tomatoes, Chopped
- ¼ Cup Tomato Puree
- ¾ Cup Vegetable Broth
- ½ Tablespoon Lemon Juice, Fresh
- ¼ Teaspoon Red Pepper Flakes, Crushed
- Sea Salt & Black Pepper to Taste

Directions:

1. Put your oil into your instant pot, pressing sauté. Add in your onion, cooking for three minutes.
2. Add in your red pepper flakes and garlic, cooking for a minute.
3. Add in your spinach, cooking for another two minutes.
4. Press cancel, and then stir in the remaining ingredients.
5. Cook on high pressure for six minutes, and then use a quick release. Serve warm.

Creamy Corn

Serves: 2

Time: 20 Minutes

Ingredients:

- 30 Ounces Canned Corn, Drained
- ½ Cup Milk
- 4 Ounces Cream Cheese
- ½ Stick Butter
- ½ Tablespoon Sugar
- Sea Salt & Black Pepper to Taste

Directions:

1. Mix all of your ingredients together and cook on low pressure for ten minutes.
2. Serve warm.

Bell Pepper Stir Fry

Serves: 2

Times: 25 Minutes

Ingredients:

- 2 Red Bell Peppers, Sliced into Strips
- 1 Tablespoon Olive Oil
- ½ Teaspoon Cumin Seeds
- 4 Small Potatoes, Cubed
- 1 Tablespoon Water
- ½ Teaspoon Dry Mango Powder
- 3 Cloves Garlic, Minced
- 1 Tablespoon Cilantro
- ¼ Teaspoon Turmeric
- ½ Teaspoon Cayenne Pepper
- 2 Teaspoons Coriander Powder

Directions:

1. Press sauté, and then let your oil heat up.
2. Add in your cumin and garlic, cooking for a minute.
3. Add in your bell peppers, turmeric, water, potatoes, cayenne and coriander. Stir well, and cook on high pressure for two minutes. Use a quick release.
4. Add in your cilantro and mango powder, and mix well. Serve warm.

Garlic & Wine Mushrooms

Serves: 2

Time: 18 Minutes

Ingredients:

- 1 ½ Tablespoons Olive Oil
- 2 Cloves Garlic, Minced
- ½ lb. Mushrooms, Sliced
- 1 ½ Tablespoons Balsamic Vinegar
- 1 ½ Tablespoons White Wine
- Sea Salt & Black Pepper to Taste

Directions:

1. Press sauté, heating your oil up in your instant pot.
2. Add in your mushrooms and garlic, cooking for three minutes. Remember to stir so it doesn't burn.
3. Add in your vinegar and wine, stirring well.
4. Cook on high pressure for two minutes, and then use a quick release.
5. Season with salt and pepper before serving.

Squash & Zucchini Medley

Serves: 2

Time: 18 Minutes

Ingredients:

- ½ Teaspoon Italian Seasoning
- 1 Cup Yellow Squash, Peeled & Sliced & Chopped
- 1 Cup Zucchini, Sliced
- ½ Teaspoon Garlic
- Sea Salt & Black Pepper to Taste
- 2 Tablespoons Butter
- ½ Cup Vegetable Stock
- 2 Tablespoons Parmesan, Grated
- 2 Tablespoons Pork Rinds, Crushed

Directions:

1. Press sauté, heating up your garlic.
2. Add in your squash, zucchini, and season. Stir and sauté for five minutes.
3. Add in your stock, cooking on low pressure for one minute.
4. Use a quick release, and then add in your pork rinds and parmesan.
5. Serve warm.

Asparagus & Mushrooms

Serves: 2

Time: 15 Minutes

Ingredients:

- ½ lb. Asparagus Crowns
- 4 Tablespoons Mushrooms, Sliced
- 3 Tablespoons Chicken Stock
- Sea Salt & Black Pepper to Taste

Directions:

1. Mix all of your ingredients in your instant pot, cooking on low pressure for two minutes.
2. Serve warm.

Cranberry Side

Serves: 2

Time: 20 Minutes

Ingredients:

- ½ lb. Cranberries, Fresh
- ½ Cup Sugar
- 2 Tablespoons Lime Zest, Grated Fresh
- ½ Orange, Juiced

Directions:

1. Mix all of your ingredients into your instant pot, and cook on high pressure for seven minutes.
2. Use a quick release and serve warm.

Spiced Okra

Serves: 2

Time: 22 Minutes

Ingredients:

- 1 Onion, Sliced
- 1 Tablespoons Olive Oil
- 3 Cloves Garlic, Chopped
- ½ Teaspoon Cumin Seeds
- 1 Tomato, Chopped
- 1 lb. Okra, Cut into 1 Inch Pieces
- ½ Cup Water
- ½ Teaspoon Coriander, Ground
- ¼ Teaspoon Turmeric
- ¼ Teaspoon Red Chili Powder
- Sea Salt & Black Pepper to Taste

Directions:

1. Put your oil in your instant pot, and press sauté. Add in your cumin and garlic, cooking for a full minute.
2. Add in your onions, cooking for another four minutes.
3. Add in your remaining ingredients, cooking for another minute.
4. Press cancel, and stir well.
5. Secure your lid, and cook on high pressure for two minutes.
6. Use a quick release, serving warm.

Zucchini & Mushrooms

Serves: 2

Time: 18 Minutes

Ingredients:

- ½ Tablespoon Olive Oil
- 1 Clove Garlic, Minced
- 1 Cup Yellow Onion, Chopped
- 1 Teaspoon Basil
- 4 Ounces Mushrooms, Sliced
- 2 Zucchinis, Sliced
- Sea Salt & Black Pepper to Taste
- 2 Zucchinis, Sliced
- 5 Ounces Tomatoes with Juice, Crushed

Directions:

1. Put your oil in the instant pot, pressing sauté. Let your oil heat up before adding in your onion, mushrooms and garlic. Stir well, and cook for four minutes.
2. Season with salt, pepper and basil. Stir well, and then add in your zucchinis. Make sure to toss to coat.
3. Add in your tomatoes, and then cook on low pressure for one minute.
4. Use a quick release before serving warm.

Garlic Bell Peppers

Serves: 2

Time: 25 Minutes

Ingredients:

- 1 Tablespoon Olive Oil
- 4 Cloves Garlic, Minced
- 1 Jalapeno Pepper, Seeded & Chopped
- 1 Green Bell Pepper, Seeded & Cut into Strips
- 1 Red Bell Pepper, Needed & Cut into Strips
- 1 Yellow Bell Pepper, Seeded & Cut into Strips
- 1 Orange Bell Pepper, Seeded & Cut into Strips
- ¼ Cup Water
- 1 Tablespoon Lemon Juice, Fresh
- Sea Salt & Black Pepper to Taste

Directions:

1. Put your oil in the instant pot, pressing sauté. Add in your jalapeno and garlic, cooking for a minute before pressing cancel. Add in all ingredients except your lemon juice.
2. Cook on high pressure for two minutes.
3. Use a quick release, and press sauté.
4. Stir in your lemon juice, cooking for another two minutes. Serve warm.

Green Beans with Bacon

Serves: 2

Time: 15 Minutes

Ingredients:

- ½ lb. Green Beans, Trimmed
- 1 Cup Water
- 2 Tablespoons Bacon, Chopped
- 2 Teaspoons Butter
- Sea Salt & Black Pepper to Taste

Directions:

1. Place your water in your instant pot before adding in your steamer basket. Fill your steamer basket with your green beans, and cook on high pressure for three minutes.
2. Use a quick release, and transfer your green beans to a bowl. Add all ingredients into your bowl, making sure your butter is melted. Toss before serving.

Spicy Zucchini

Serves: 2

Time: 12 Minutes

Ingredients:

- 1/3 Cup Water
- 2 Zucchinis, Sliced
- ½ Tablespoon butter
- 1 Tablespoon Cajun Seasoning
- ½ Teaspoon Smoked Paprika
- ½ Teaspoon Garlic Powder

Directions:

1. Mix all ingredients into your instant pot, cooking on high pressure for one minute.
2. Use a quick release and serve warm.

Green Beans & Mushrooms

Serves: 2

Time: 37 Minutes

Ingredients:

- ½ lb. Green Beans, Fresh & Trimmed
- ½ Tablespoons Butter
- 4 Ounces Bacon, Chopped
- ½ Onion, Small & Chopped
- 1 Clove Garlic, Minced
- 4 Ounces Mushrooms, Fresh & Sliced
- 1 Teaspoon Red Wine Vinegar
- Sea Salt & Black Pepper to Taste

Directions:

1. Add your green beans to your instant pot with enough water to cover them.
2. Cook on high pressure for two minutes, and then use a quick release.
3. Remove the lid, and drain your green beans using a colander.
4. Remove your water from your instant pot, drying it out.
5. Add your butter into the instant pot, and press sauté. Add in your bacon, and cook for three to four more minutes.
6. Add in your garlic and onion, cooking for two minutes.
7. Add in your mushrooms, cooking for six more minutes.
8. Stir in your vinegar, salt, black pepper, and green beans. Cook for a minute before pressing cancel. Serve warm.

Mexican Zucchini

Serves: 2

Time: 25 Minutes

Ingredients:

- 1 Teaspoon Butter
- 1 Yellow Onion, Small & Chopped
- 1 Poblano Pepper, Sliced Thin
- ½ Tablespoon Olive Oil
- ½ Tablespoon Garlic, Minced
- ½ Zucchini, Chopped Rough
- ½ Yellow Squash, Peeled & Chopped Rough
- Sea Salt & Black Pepper to Taste
- 3 Tablespoons Chicken Stock
- ½ Tablespoon Sour Cream
- ¼ Teaspoon Cumin

Directions:

1. Press sauté and heat up your oil.
2. Add in your poblano strips, and stir. Cook for ten minutes.
3. Add in your garlic, onion and butter. Stir well, cooking for another two minutes.
4. Add zucchini, squash, salt, pepper, stock and cumin. Stir well, and cook on low pressure for two minutes.
5. Use a quick release, and then add in sour cream. Toss to coat, and then serve warm.

Comfort Food Recipes!

If you're looking for comfort food, look no further. This chapter is dedicated to comforting meals made easy. You'll find many old favorites in this chapter.

Apple Crisp

Serves: 2

Time: 25 Minutes

Ingredients:

- 1/3 Cup Old Fashioned Rolled Oats
- 2 Tablespoons Flour
- 2 Tablespoons Butter, Melted
- 2 Tablespoons Brown Sugar
- 1/8 Teaspoon Sea Salt, Fine
- 2 ½ Apples, Peeled, Cored & Chunked
- 1 Teaspoon Cinnamon
- ¼ Teaspoon Nutmeg
- 1 Cup Water
- ½ Tablespoon Honey

Directions:

1. Mix your butter, flour, brown sugar, oats and salt together.
2. Place your apple chunks in the bottom of your instant pot, sprinkling with cinnamon and nutmeg.
3. Add in your honey and water.
4. Drop your oat mixture on top of the apples by the spoonful.
5. Cook on high pressure for eight minutes, and then allow for a natural pressure release. Serve warm.

Corn on the Cob

Serves: 2

Time: 15 Minutes

Ingredients:

- 1 Teaspoon Onion Powder
- 3 Cobs of Corn, Halved
- ½ Cup Water
- 1 ½ Tablespoons Butter
- 1 Clove Garlic, Minced
- 1 Teaspoon Sweet Paprika
- ¼ Teaspoon Cayenne Pepper
- 1 Teaspoon Oregano
- Sea Salt & Black Pepper to Taste
- ½ Lime, Sliced into Wedges
- 1 Tablespoon Cilantro, Fresh & Chopped

Directions:

1. Place your water in your instant pot and lower in your steamer basket with your corn inside. Cook on high pressure for three minutes, and then use a quick release.
2. Put your corn on a plate, cleaning your instant pot out.
3. Pres sauté, and add in your butter.
4. Once your butter is melted, add in your garlic. Stir and cook for about half a minute.
5. Add all remaining ingredients except your lime wedges and cilantro. Stir well, and cook for another two minutes.
6. Garnish with cilantro and lime wedges before serving.

Chocolate Cake

Serves: 2

Time: 18 Minutes

Ingredients:

- 1 Egg
- 4 Tablespoons Flour
- 4 Tablespoons Milk
- 4 Tablespoons Sugar
- 2 Tablespoons Olive Oil
- Pinch Sea Salt, Fine
- 1 Tablespoon Cocoa Powder
- ½ Teaspoon Orange Zest
- ½ Teaspoon Baking Powder
- 1 Cup Water

Directions:

1. Mix all of your ingredients together, and make sure to stir well.
2. Grease two ramekins, and add your water into your instant pot.
3. Add your steamer basket in, and then cook on high pressure for six minutes.
4. Use a quick release and serve warm.

Collard Greens with Bacon

Serves: 2

Time: 40 Minutes

Ingredients:

- ½ lb. Collard Greens, Trimmed
- 1 Cup Bacon, Chopped
- 4 Tablespoons Water
- Sea Salt & Black Pepper to Taste

Directions:

1. Press sauté, cooking your bacon for five minutes in your instant pot.
2. Add in all of your other ingredients, and cook on high pressure for twenty minutes.
3. Use a quick release, and serve warm.

Southern Collard Greens

Serves: 2

Time: 18 Minutes

Ingredients:

- ½ Yellow Onion, Chopped Rough
- 1 Bunch Collard Greens, Trimmed & Cut into Medium Strips
- 1 Tablespoon Water
- 2 Cloves Garlic, Minced
- ½ Cup Water
- Sea Salt to Taste
- ¼ Teaspoon Red Pepper Flakes

Directions:

1. Press sauté, and add in your water and onions. Stir well and cook for two minutes.
2. Add your salt, garlic and red pepper flakes. Stir and cook for a minute more.
3. Add in your collard greens with another cup of water.
4. Cook on high pressure for three minutes before using a quick release. Serve warm.

Carrot Cake

Serves: 2

Time: 40 Minutes

Ingredients:

- ¼ Teaspoon Baking Soda
- ¼ Teaspoon Baking Powder
- 2 Ounces Flour
- ¼ Teaspoon Cinnamon
- Pinch Ground Nutmeg
- Pinch Allspice
- 2 Cups Water
- 1 Egg
- 1 Tablespoon Yogurt
- 2 Tablespoons Sugar
- 2 Tablespoons Pineapple Juice
- 2 Tablespoons Carrots, Grated
- 2 Tablespoons Coconut Oil, Melted
- 2 Tablespoons Pecans, Toasted & Chopped
- 2 Tablespoons Coconut Flakes

Directions:

1. Mix all cake ingredients together before pouring them into a greased cake pan.
2. Add your water into your instant pot, adding in your steamer basket add in your cake pan on top, and cook on high pressure for thirty-two minutes.

Chocolate Pudding

Serves: 2
Time: 30 Minutes
Ingredients:

- 3 Ounces Chocolate, Chopped
- 3 Tablespoons Milk
- 3 Egg Yolks
- 1 Cup Heavy Cream
- 3 Tablespoons Brown Sugar
- 1 Teaspoon Vanilla Extract
- 1 ½ Cups Water
- Pinch Ground Cardamom
- Crème Fraiche for Serving

Directions:

1. Place your milk and cream in a pot, bringing it to a simmer over medium heat. Add in your chocolate, and whisk until well combined.
2. In a bowl mix your vanilla, sugar, egg yolks and cardamom. Stir well before straining.
3. Mix with your chocolate, and transfer to two soufflé dishes. Cover your dishes with tin foil, and place your water into your instant pot.
4. Add in your steamer basket, and then put your soufflé dishes on top.
5. Cook on low pressure for eighteen minutes, and then use a quick release.
6. Allow your pudding to cool before serving with cream fraiche.

Roasted Potatoes

Serves: 2

Time: 25 Minutes

Ingredients:

- ½ Teaspoon Garlic
- ¼ Teaspoon Onion
- ½ lb. Potatoes, Cut into Wedges
- 2 Tablespoons Avocado Oil
- Sea Salt & Black Pepper to Taste
- ½ Cup Chicken Stock

Directions:

1. Add in your oil and press sauce.
2. Toss in your garlic, onion powder, potatoes, salt and pepper. Stir, and cook for eight minutes.
3. Add in your stock, cooking on high pressure for seven minutes.
4. Serve warm.

Apple Cobbler

Serves: 2
Time: 25 Minutes
Ingredients:

- ½ Pear, Cored & Chopped
- ½ Plum, Stone Removed & Chopped
- ½ Apple, Cored & Chopped
- 1 Tablespoon Honey
- ¼ Teaspoon Cinnamon
- 1 ½ Tablespoons Coconut Oil
- 1 Cup Water
- 2 Tablespoons Pecans, Chopped
- 2 Tablespoons Coconut, Shredded
- 1 Tablespoon Sunflower Seeds

Directions:

1. Put your fruit in a dish, adding in your cinnamon, honey and coconut oil. Toss to coat.
2. Add your water to the instant pot before adding your steamer basket. Place your dish inside, and cook on high pressure for ten minutes. Use a quick release.
3. In the same baking dish mix your pecans, sunflower seeds and coconut. Stir well, and then place it back into the instant pot.
4. Cook on high pressure for two minutes, and then use a quick release.
5. Dust with cinnamon before serving.

Easy Shrimp

Serves: 2
Time: 15 Minutes
Ingredients:

- 1 Tablespoon Butter
- 1 Tablespoon Olive Oil
- 1 lb. Shrimp
- ½ Tablespoon Garlic, Minced
- ¼ Cup White Wine
- ¼ Cup Chicken Stock
- 1 Tablespoon Parsley, Chopped
- ½ Tablespoon Lemon Juice
- Sea Salt & Black Pepper to Taste

Directions:

1. Press sauté, and then add in your butter and oil. Once they're heated up, add in your garlic, cooking for a minute.
2. Add in your wine and stock. Stir well, and then add in your parsley and shrimp. Cook on high pressure for two minutes. Use a quick release.
3. Serve warm and with pasta if desired.

Onion Soup

Serves: 2

Time: 35 Minutes

Ingredients:

- 1 Tablespoon Avocado Oil
- ½ Tablespoon Balsamic Vinegar
- 4 Cups Yellow Onion, Chopped
- 3 Cups Pork Stock
- Sea Salt & Black Pepper to Taste
- 1 Bay Leaf
- 1 Thyme Sprig, Chopped

Directions:

1. Press sauté, and then add in your oil. Allow it to heat up, and then add in your onion.
2. Season with salt and pepper, and sauté for fifteen minutes. Make sure to stir so it doesn't burn.
3. Add in your thyme, bay leaf, vinegar and stock. Cook on high pressure for ten minutes.
4. Discard your bay leaf and blend using the immersion blender.

Potato Soup

Serves: 2

Time: 40 Minutes

Ingredients:

- 1 Carrot, Chopped
- 4 Potatoes, Peeled & Cubed
- 4 Ounces Roasted Garlic Paste
- 3 Tablespoons Celery, Chopped
- 2 Tablespoons Baby Spinach Leaves, Chopped
- 1 Yellow Onion, Chopped
- ½ Cup Chicken Stock
- Sea Salt & Black Pepper
- Pinch Smoked Paprika
- ½ Tablespoon Chia Seeds
- Pinch Red Pepper, Crushed

Directions:

1. Mix your potatoes, carrot, garlic paste, celery, spinach, onion, stock, salt, pepper, chia seeds, red pepper, and paprika. Stir well.
2. Cook on soup mode for a half hour.
3. Blend using an immersion blender, and serve warm.

Pork Roast

Serves: 2

Time: 45 Minutes

Ingredients:

- Sea Salt & Black Pepper to Taste
- Pinch Garlic
- Pinch Chili Powder
- Pinch Onion Powder
- 1 lb. Pork Roast
- ½ Tablespoon Olive Oil
- 3 Tablespoons Apple Juice
- 1 Cup Water

Directions:

1. Mix all of your spices into a bowl and then rub your roast down with it.
2. Press sauté and allow your oil to heat up add in your roast, browning for five minutes per side.
3. Add in your water and apple juice, cooking on high pressure for twenty-five minutes.
4. Slice your roast, and drizzle with juices to serve.

Simple Lasagna

Serves: 2

Time: 15 Minutes

Ingredients:

- 6 Ounces Ruffles Pasta
- ¼ lb. Ground Beef
- ¼ lb. Ground Pork
- 4 Ounces Ricotta Cheese
- 4 Ounces Mozzarella Cheese
- 1 Cup Pasta Sauce
- 1 Cup Water

Directions:

1. Press sauté, and then add in your pork and beef. Brown it, making sure that your meat is crumbled.
2. Add in your pasta, water and sauce, and then cook on high pressure for five minutes.
3. Use quick release, and then add in half of your mozzarella and ricotta. Mix well.
4. Serve topped with your remaining mozzarella.

Chicken Wings

Serves: 2

Time: 30 Minutes

Ingredients:

- ¼ Cup Tomato Paste
- 1 ½ lbs. Chicken Wings
- 1 Tablespoon Honey, Raw
- 1 Tablespoon Lemon Juice, Fresh
- Sea Salt & Black Pepper to Taste

Directions:

1. Put your trivet into your instant pot, adding a cup of water into your instant pot.
2. Put your chicken wings on a trivet, and then cook on high pressure for ten minutes.
3. Use a quick release, and then preheat our oven broiler.
4. Get out a bowl, and add all of your remaining ingredients. Beat well, and then transfer the chicken wings into your bowl of sauce.
5. Coat your wings generously, and then place them on a baking sheet that's been lined with parchment paper. Broil for five minutes, and serve with remaining sauce.

Strawberry Shortcake

Serves: 2
Time: 45 Minutes
Ingredients:

- 1 Cup White Flour
- 1 Cup Water
- 3 Tablespoons Sugar
- ½ Teaspoon Baking Powder
- ¼ Teaspoon Baking Soda
- 3 Tablespoons Butter
- ½ Cup Buttermilk
- 1 ½ Tablespoons Sugar
- 1 Egg, Whisked
- 1 Cup Strawberries, Sliced
- ½ Tablespoon Mint, Chopped
- ½ Teaspoon Lime Zest
- ½ Tablespoon Rum

Directions:

1. Mix your flour, two tablespoons sugar, baking soda and baking powder together. Stir well.
2. Get out another bowl and mix your egg and buttermilk together. Stir well before adding it into your flour mixture. Whisk well.
3. Spoon this dough into two greased jars, and cover your jars with tin foil.
4. Add your water to your instant pot, and then place in your steamer basket. Add your jars onto your steamer basket, and then cook on high pressure for twenty-five minutes. Use a quick release when done.
5. While this cooks get out another bowl and mix your strawberries with a tablespoon of sugar. Add in your mint, rum and lime zest. Toss to make sure everything is coated.
6. Serve your cakes with your strawberry mix.

Spinach Dip

Serves: 2

Time: 12 Minutes

Ingredients:

- 3 Cloves Garlic, Minced
- 1 lb. Spinach, Fresh
- 1 Tablespoon Olive Oil
- ½ Cup Chicken Broth
- ½ Cup Sour Cream
- 8 Ounces Cream Cheese, Cubed
- ½ Cup Mayonnaise
- 1 Cup Mozzarella Cheese, Shredded
- 1 Teaspoon Onion Powder
- Sea Salt & Black Pepper to Taste

Directions:

1. Press the sauté button, combining your garlic and spinach together. Cook until your spinach has wilted, and then drain away any excess liquid.
2. Leave the spinach and garlic in your pot, adding in your sour cream, cream cheese, chicken broth, mozzarella and mayonnaise. Stir well, and season with onion powder.
3. Add the lid, and cook on high pressure for ten minutes.
4. Use a quick release and season with salt and pepper before serving.

Dessert Recipes

Your instant pot can be used for dessert too! In this chapter you'll find a little something for everyone.

Blueberry Custard

Serves: 2

Time: 30 Minutes

Ingredients:

- ¼ Cup Blueberries
- 2 Teaspoons Confectioner's Sugar
- ¼ Teaspoon Vanilla Extract, Pure
- 1/8 Teaspoon Sea Salt, Fine
- ¼ Teaspoon Ground Nutmeg
- 3 Tablespoons All Purpose Flour
- 1 Tablespoon Honey, Raw
- 2 Eggs
- 1 Tablespoon Butter, Melted
- ¾ Cups Milk

Directions:

1. Add your butter to your baking dish, making sure it's covered.
2. Blend your honey, milk, eggs, flour, salt and vanilla together. Make sure it's smooth, and then pour it into a prepared dish.
3. Sprinkle your blueberries on top, and then add two cups of water into your instant pot.
4. Place your trivet into your instant pot, and then put your dish on top.
5. Cook on high pressure for twenty-five minutes. Allow for a natural pressure release.
6. Sprinkle with confectioner's sugar and nutmeg before serving.

Banana Foster

Serves: 2

Time: 1 Hour 10 Minutes

Ingredients:

- 2 Bananas, Peeled & Sliced
- 2 Tablespoons Butter, Melted
- ½ Cup Brown Sugar, Packed
- 2 Tablespoons Rum
- ½ Teaspoon Vanilla Extract
- 2 Tablespoons Walnuts, chopped
- ½ Teaspoon Cinnamon
- 2 Tablespoons Coconut, Shredded

Directions:

1. Slice your banana and place it at the bottom of your instant pot.
2. Get out a bowl and whisk together your brown sugar, butter, rum, vanilla extract and cinnamon.
3. Pour this mixture over your bananas, and then slow cook for an hour.
4. Sprinkle with walnuts and coconut before serving warm.

Lemon Pudding

Serves: 2

Time: 40 Minutes

Ingredients:

- ½ Cup Milk
- ½ Lemon, Zested
- 3 Egg Yolks
- ½ Cup Fresh Cream
- 1 Cup Water
- 3 Tablespoons Sugar
- Blackberry Syrup to Serve

Directions:

1. Place a pan over medium heat, adding in your cream, lemon zest and milk. Stir well.
2. Bring this mixture to a boil before taking it off heat. Allow it to settle for thirty minutes.
3. In a bowl mix your sugar, egg yolks and cream mixture.
4. Stir well, and get out two ramekins. Cream your ramekins and pour in your pudding mixture.
5. Cover your ramekins with tinfoil and add your water to your instant pot. Add in your steamer basket, and then place your ramekins on top.
6. Cook on high pressure for ten minutes. Use a quick release, and then serve with blackberry syrup.

Cranberry Bread Pudding

Serves: 2

Time: 25 Minutes

Ingredients:

- 2 Egg Yolks
- 1 ½ Cups Bread, Cubed
- 1 Cup Heavy Cream
- ½ Orange, Zested & Juiced
- 2 Teaspoons Vanilla Extract
- ½ Cup Sugar
- 2 Cups Water
- 1 Tablespoon Butter
- ½ Cup Cranberries

Directions:

1. Add all ingredients together except for your water. Mix well
2. Put your water in your instant pot, and then add in your steamer basket. Add your baking dish in.
3. Cook on high pressure for fifteen minutes, and serve cold.

Cranberry & Apricot Pudding

Serves: 2

Time: 45 Minutes

Ingredients:

- 2 Ounces Apricots, Chopped
- 2 Cups Water
- 1 Teaspoon Olive Oil
- 2 Ounces Cranberries, Dried & Soaked in Hot Water, Drained & Chopped
- 2 Cups Water
- ½ Cup White Flour
- 1 ½ Teaspoons Baking Powder
- ½ Cup Sugar
- ½ Teaspoon Ginger
- Pinch Cinnamon Powder
- 2 Eggs
- 7 Tablespoons Butter
- 1 Carrot, Small & Grated
- 1 ½ Tablespoons Maple Syrup

Directions:

1. Blend all ingredients together, and spread it into a pudding mold. Make sure that your pudding mold is greased first.
2. Add your water into your instant pot, and then place your steamer basket in it.
3. Add your pudding mold in it, and then cook on high pressure for thirty-five minutes.
4. Allow it to cool down before serving.

Apple Cake

Serves: 2

Time: 1 Hour 10 Minutes

Ingredients:

- 1 Egg
- ½ Tablespoon Apple Pie Spice
- ½ Tablespoon Vanilla Extract
- ½ Cup Sugar
- 1 ½ Cups Apples, Cored & Cubed
- 1 Cup Flour
- ½ Tablespoon Baking Powder
- ½ Stick Butter
- 1 Cup Water

Directions:

1. Mix your butter, egg, apple pie spice, apples, sugar, baking powder and flour. Stir well, and then grease a cake pan. Pour it into your cake pan.
2. Add your water, and then put in a steamer basket. Cook on high pressure for one hour.
3. Use a quick release and allow it to cool before serving.

Sweet Rice Pudding

Serves: 2

Time: 25 Minutes

Ingredients:

- ½ Cup Brown Rice
- 1 Cup Water
- 3 Tablespoons Coconut Chips
- ½ Cup Coconut Milk
- 3 Tablespoons Maple Syrup
- 2 Tablespoons Raisins
- 2 Tablespoons Almonds, Chopped
- Pinch Cinnamon Powder

Directions:

1. Place your rice and water in your instant pot, and then cook on high pressure for twelve minutes. Use a quick release.
2. Add in your remaining ingredients and stir well.
3. Cook on high pressure for five minutes, and then use a quick release.
4. Serve chilled.

Black Rice Pudding

Serves: 2

Time: 45 Minutes

Ingredients:

- 3 Cups Water
- 1 Cup Black Rice
- 3 Tablespoons Sugar
- 1 Cinnamon Stick
- 2 Cardamom Pods, Crushed
- 1 Clove
- 2 Tablespoons Mango, Chopped
- 3 Tablespoons Coconut, Grated

Directions:

1. Place your rice and water into your instant pot. Add in your cinnamon, cardamom and clove. Cook on low pressure for twenty-five minutes and then use a quick release.
2. Discard your cardamom, clove and cinnamon. Add in our coconut and press sauté.
3. Cook for ten minutes, and serve topped with mango.

Caramel Pudding

Serves: 2

Time: 40 Minutes

Ingredients:

- ½ Teaspoon Baking Powder
- 2 Tablespoons White Sugar
- ½ Cup White Flour
- ¼ Teaspoon Cinnamon
- 2 Tablespoon Butter
- 4 Tablespoons Milk
- 3 Tablespoons Pecans, Chopped
- 1 ½ Cups Water
- 3 Tablespoons Raisins
- 3 Tablespoons Orange Zest
- 3 Tablespoons Orange Juice
- 3 Tablespoons Brown Sugar
- Caramel Topping

Directions:

1. Mix your white sugar, baking powder, cinnamon and flour together. Stir well.
2. Add in half of your butter and milk, stirring again.
3. Add in your raisins and pecans, stirring again.
4. Grease a pudding pan, pouring your mixture into it.
5. Heat up a pan over medium high heat, adding in half a cup of water, orange juice, orange zest, your remaining butter and brown sugar. Stir well, bringing it to a boil for two minutes. Pour this mixture over your pudding.
6. Add a cup of water to your instant pot before adding in your trivet.
7. Cook on high pressure for twenty minutes. Use a quick release.
8. Serve with caramel topping.

Black Tea Cake

Serves: 2

Time: 40 Minutes

Ingredients:

- 2 Tablespoons Black Tea Powder
- ½ Cup Milk
- 1 Tablespoon Butter
- 2 Eggs
- 1 Cup Sugar
- 1 Teaspoon Vanilla Extract, Pure
- 3 Tablespoons Coconut Oil
- 2 Cups Flour
- ¼ Teaspoon Baking Soda
- 2 Cups Water
- 1 Teaspoon Baking Powder

Cream:

- 1 ½ Tablespoons Honey, Raw
- ¼ Cup Butter, Soft
- 1 ½ Cups Sugar

Directions:

1. Place your tea and milk into a pot, warming it over medium heat. Stake it off the stove, and then allow it to cool down.
2. Mix a tablespoon of butter, one cup of sugar, oil, vanilla extract, eggs, baking soda, baking powder, and two cups of flour into a bowl. Stir well, and pour it into a prepared greased pan.
3. Add the water into your instant pot, and then place in your steamer basket. Add your cake pan on top, and cook on high pressure for thirty minutes.
4. In a bowl mix together one and a half cups of sugar, one quarter cup of butter and honey. Whisk well, and allow it to cool before serving.

Lava Cakes

Serves: 2

Time: 15 Minutes

Ingredients:

- ½ Tablespoon Sugar
- 2 Ounces Semi-Sweet Chocolate, Chopped
- ¼ Cup Butter
- 1 Egg Yolk
- 1 Egg
- ½ Teaspoon Instant Coffee
- ½ Cup Confectioner's Sugar
- ½ Teaspoon Vanilla Extract, Pure
- 1/8 Teaspoon Sea Salt, Fine
- 3 Tablespoons All Purpose Flour

Directions:

1. Grease two ramekins before coating them with sugar.
2. Get out a bowl and melt your butter and chocolate together before adding in your confectioner's sugar.
3. Whisk your egg yolk, egg, coffee and vanilla. Add in your salt and flour.
4. Divide this mixture into your ramekin, and pour two cups of water into your instant pot before adding in your trivet. Put your ramekins on the trivet.
5. Cook on high pressure for nine minutes before using a quick release.
6. Dust your cakes with powdered sugar before serving.

Green Tea Pudding

Serves: 2

Time: 15 Minutes

Ingredients:

- 7 Ounces Milk
- 7 Ounces Heavy Cream
- 1 Tablespoon Green Tea Powder
- 1 ½ Tablespoons Sugar
- ½ Teaspoon Honey, Raw

Directions:

1. Mix your milk and green tea powder in your instant pot. Add in your sugar, honey and heavy cream. Stir well, and then cook on high pressure for three minutes.
2. Allow to cool before serving.

Glazed Pears

Serves: 2

Time: 25 Minutes

Ingredients:

- 6 Ounce Currant Jelly
- 13 Ounce Grape Jelly
- 1 Tablespoon Lemon Juice, Fresh
- ½ Teaspoon Lemon Zest, Grated
- 2 Pears
- 2 Peppercorns
- ¼ Vanilla Bean
- 1 Rosemary Sprig

Directions:

1. Mix your grape juice, jelly, and lemon juice and lemon zest.
2. Dip each pear into your juice mixture, making sure that it's coated.
3. Wrap each pear in foil.
4. Add your rosemary, vanilla bean, and peppercorn.
5. Put a steamer basket over the liquid, putting your pears inside.
6. Cook on high pressure for ten minutes.
7. Use a quick release, and unwrap your pears. Top with cooking liquid to serve.

Millet Pudding

Serves: 2

Time: 20 Minutes

Ingredients:

- 3 Ounces Water
- 7 Ounces Milk
- ½ Cup Millet
- 4 Dates, Pitted
- Honey for Serving

Directions:

1. Place your millet in your instant pot, adding in your water, milk and dates. Cook on high pressure for ten minutes. Use a quick release.
2. Divide between bowls and top with honey before serving.

Cranberry Bowl

Serves: 2

Time: 40 Minutes

Ingredients:

Sauce:

- ¼ Teaspoon Cinnamon
- 1 Cup Cranberries
- 2 Tablespoons Orange Juice
- 3 Tablespoons Sugar

Bowls:

- 1 Cup Milk
- 3 Tablespoons Sugar
- 1 Egg, Whisked
- 2 Tablespoons Butter, Melted
- ½ Teaspoon Vanilla Extract, Pure
- ½ Bread Loaf, Cubed
- ½ Cup Water
- ½ Orange, Zested

Directions:

1. Press sauté and add in your orange juice, cinnamon, three tablespoons of sugar and cranberries. Stir well, cooking for five minutes. Transfer this mixture to a greased pan.
2. Get out a bowl and mix your butter and milk. Add in three tablespoons of sugar, egg, vanilla extract, read cubes and orange zest. Stir well, and pour it into your greased pan as well.
3. Add in your water, and then place in your steamer basket. Add the pan inside, and cook on high pressure for twenty-five minutes. Use a quick release.
4. Divide into dessert bowls before serving.

Sweetened Chia Pudding

Serves: 2

Time: 15 Minutes

Ingredients:

- 4 Teaspoons Sugar
- 2 Tablespoons Coconut, Shredded
- 2 Tablespoons Almonds
- 4 Tablespoons Chia Seeds
- 1 Cup Almond Milk

Directions:

1. Place all of your ingredients into the instant pot, cooking on high pressure for three minutes.
2. Use a quick release, and divide between bowls to serve. You can also serve your pudding chilled.

Pumpkin Cake

Serves: 2
Time: 55 Minutes
Ingredients:

- ¼ Teaspoon Baking Soda
- ½ Cup Whole Wheat Flour
- ½ Cup White Flour
- ¼ Teaspoon Pumpkin Pie Spice
- 1 Banana, Mashed
- 3 Tablespoons Sugar
- 2 Tablespoons Greek Yogurt
- ½ Tablespoons Canola Oil
- 2 Ounces Pumpkin Puree, Canned
- 1 Quart Water
- 1 Egg
- ¼ Teaspoon Vanilla Extract, Pure
- 2 Tablespoons Chocolate Chips

Directions:

1. Mix your flours together with your baking soda, pumpkin pie spice, baking powder and salt. Stir well.
2. Add in your oil, banana, yogurt, sugar, pumpkin puree, vanilla and egg. Stir well.
3. Add in your chocolate chips, and stir again
4. Grease a cake pan with cooking spray, adding in your batter.
5. Place your water into your instant pot, and then add your steamer basket in.
6. Add in your cake pan, and then cook on high pressure for thirty-five minutes.
7. Allow it to cool before serving.

Pumpkin Pudding

Serves: 2

Time: 50 Minutes

Ingredients:

- 1/3 Cup Pumpkin Puree, Canned & Drained Well
- 1 Teaspoon Gelatin
- ¼ Cup Coconut Milk
- ½ Egg
- ¼ Cup Coconut Sugar
- ¼ Teaspoon Allspice
- ½ Teaspoon Cinnamon
- 1/8 Teaspoon Ginger
- 1/8 Teaspoon Nutmeg
- 1/8 Teaspoon Ground Cloves
- Pinch Sea Salt, Fine
- ½ Cup Water

Directions:

1. Add your milk in a pan over medium-low heat and sprinkle with gelatin. Make sure it's heated all the way through and beat continuously. Remove from heat, setting it to the side.
2. In a bowl add this mixture ty our egg, pumpkin, coconut sugar, spices, and salt. Beat until smooth.
3. Grease a soufflé dish, and transfer your mixture into your dish.
4. Add a cup of water and ten place your trivet in. arrange your dish on top, and cook on high pressure for a half hour.
5. Use a quick release, and allow to cool completely on a wire rack.
6. Refrigerate for four to six hours before serving.

Strawberry Cobbler

Serves: 2

Time: 30 Minutes

Ingredients:

- 1 ¼ Cup All Purpose Flour
- ¾ Cup Milk
- 1 ½ Teaspoons Baking Powder
- ½ Cup Granulated Sugar
- 1/3 Cup Butter, Softened
- 1 Teaspoon Vanilla Extract
- ¾ Cup Strawberries, Fresh, Hulled & Sliced

Directions:

1. Mix all ingredients except for your strawberries in a bowl. Whisk well, and mix until combined.
2. Fold in your strawberry slices, and then grease your pan.
3. Pour your mixture into the pan, and add a cup of water to your instant pot. Place your trivet in, putting your pan on the trivet.
4. Cook on high pressure for twelve minutes, and then allow for a natural pressure release for five minutes. Use a quick release for the remaining pressure.
5. Allow to cool before serving.

Caramel Flan

Serves: 2

Time: 30 Minutes

Ingredients:

Caramel:

- 1/3 Cup Sugar
- 3 Tablespoons Water

Flan:

- 2 Eggs
- 1 Egg Yolk
- 3 Tablespoons Sugar
- Pinch Sea Salt
- 1 Cup Milk
- ¼ Cup Whipping Cream
- 1 Tablespoon Hazelnut Syrup
- ½ Teaspoon Vanilla Extract, Pure

Directions:

1. Get out a pan for your caramel and add in your water and sugar. Place it over medium high heat, and then bring it to a boil make sure to stir constantly and cook until it turns a dark golden brown.
2. Put your caramel into two custard cups, spreading it out evenly. Your custard cups should be six ounces eat, and allow them to cool.
3. To make your flan, mi your eggs, egg yolk, salt and sugar with a mixer. Make sure it's well combined.
4. In a pan add your milk, and heat it over medium heat it should just warm up. Add the warm milk into your egg mixture, making sure to beat continuously, and add all remaining ingredients. Mix well.
5. Put the custard into the caramel custard cups, making sure you remove all bubbles.
6. Arrange your steamer trivet in your instant pot, adding one and a half cups of water into your instant pot with your custard cups on top.
7. Cook on high pressure for six minutes, and then use a natural pressure release.
8. Allow them to cool on a wire rack, and cover the cups with plastic wrap.
9. Let them chill at least four hours before serving.

Vanilla Custard

Serves: 2

Time: 25 Minutes

Ingredients:

- 4 Egg Yolks, Large
- Pinch Sea Salt, Fine
- 1 Cup Cream
- 3 Tablespoons Granulated Sugar
- ½ Teaspoon Vanilla Extract, Pure
- ½ Teaspoon Cinnamon

Directions:

1. Add your egg yolks into a large bowl before adding in your vanilla, salt and granulated sugar. Beat until combined, and then add in your cream. Make sure it's mixed well.
2. Strain your mixture, stirring continuously, and then transfer this mixture into two large ramekins. Cover them with foil, and then place them on your trivet in your instant pot. Add in a cup and a half of water on the bottom of your instant pot.
3. Cook on high pressure for six minutes, and then use a quick release.
4. Allow your ramekins to cool on a wire rack, and ten wrap them with plastic wrap.
5. Allow them to cool in the fridge for three hours to set.
6. Sprinkle with cinnamon before serving.

Stuffed Peaches

Serves: 2
Time: 30 Minutes
Ingredients:

- 1 ½ Tablespoons Almonds
- ¾ Cup Amoretti Cookies
- 1 Tablespoons Butter, Melted
- 2 Peaches, Halved & Pitted
- ½ Teaspoon Lemon Zest, Grated Fresh
- 2 Tablespoons Sugar
- 1 Cup Red Wine

Directions:

1. Place your cookies and almonds in a food processor, processing until chopped. Transfer this mix into a bowl.
2. Add in your lemon zest and butter, pulsing.
3. Use a melon baller to make a pit in your peaches after taking out the seed.
4. Fill your peaches with your cookie mixture and.
5. Put your wine and sugar in the bottom of your instant pot, making sure to stir well. Add in your tamer basket with your peaches in the steamer basket.
6. Cook on high pressure for three minutes before using a quick release.
7. Remove your peaches and then press sauté. Cook for two to three minutes until the wine sauce thickens.
8. Serve your peaches drizzled with your wine sauce.

Banana Cake

Serves: 2

Time: 1 Hour 5 Minutes

Ingredients:

- ½ Cup Sugar
- 1 Cup Water
- 1 ½ Bananas, Peeled & Mashed
- 1 Cup Flour
- 1 Egg
- ½ Stick Butter
- ½ Teaspoon Cinnamon
- ½ Teaspoon Baking Powder
- ½ Teaspoon Nutmeg

Directions:

1. Mix all of your ingredients together before pouring them into a greased cake pan.
2. Add your water into your instant pot before adding in your steamer basket. Put the cake pan in the steamer basket, cooking on high pressure for fifty-five minutes.
3. Use a quick release and allow it to cool down before serving.

Braised Apples

Serves: 2

Time: 25 Minutes

Ingredients:

- 2 Apples, Cored
- ½ Cup Water
- 3 Tablespoon Demerara Sugar
- 2 Tablespoons Raisins
- ½ Cup Red Wine
- ½ Teaspoons Cinnamon

Directions:

1. Add your water and then put your apples in your instant pot. Pour your wine in and sprinkle with cinnamon, raisins and sugar.
2. Cook on high pressure for ten minutes before using a quick release.
3. Serve with cooking liquid.

Chocolate Bread Pudding

Serves: 2

Time: 22 Minutes

Ingredients:

- 2 Cups Challah Bread, Cubed
- ¼ Cup Milk
- 1 Egg
- ½ Teaspoon Cinnamon
- ¼ Cup Condensed Milk
- 1/3 Cup Chocolate, Chunked
- 1 Cup Water

Directions:

1. Mix your condensed milk, milk, egg and cinnamon together in a bowl.
2. Add your chocolate and bread cubes in, stirring well.
3. Divide between two ramekins, and then place your water into your instant pot. Add your trivet in, placing your ramekins on top. Cover, cooking on high pressure for eleven minutes before using a quick release.
4. Serve warm.

Fruit Cobbler

Serves: 2

Time: 20 Minutes

Ingredients:

- 1 Plum, Deseeded & Chopped
- 1 Pear, Cored & Chopped
- 1 Apple, Cored & Chopped
- 2 Tablespoons Honey, Raw
- 3 Tablespoons Coconut Oil
- ½ Teaspoon Cinnamon
- ¼ Cup Coconut, Shredded & Unsweetened
- ¼ Cup Pecans, Chopped
- 2 Tablespoons Sunflower Seeds, Roasted

Directions:

1. Mix your pear, apple, plum, honey, oil, and cinnamon together. Stir well, and over. Steam for ten minutes before transferring it to a bowl.
2. Put your sunflower seeds, coconut and pecans into your instant pot, sautéing for five minutes.
3. Sprinkle this over your fruit mix to serve.

Conclusion

Now you know everything you need to in order to start cooking simple, healthy, and delicious recipes for you and your child! The recipes in this book are meant to keep you cooking new and fun meals so that you don't get tired of eating the same thing every day. The instant pot will easily become your best friend in the kitchen, helping you to add variety and spice into your daily meals without having to slave away for hours at a time. There's no reason to settle for fast or frozen food when home cooked meals are just a few buttons away. You should never have to feed your child second best.

Learn more about Sydney Foster and her books at: http://www.KetoDiet.coach

Don't miss out!

Visit the website below and you can sign up to receive emails whenever Sydney Foster publishes a new book. There's no charge and no obligation.

https://books2read.com/r/B-A-UPAG-VSFX

BOOKS 2 READ

Connecting independent readers to independent writers.

Also by Sydney Foster

Keto Diet Coach

Ketogenic Diet Guide for Beginners: Easy Weight Loss with Plans and Recipes (Keto Cookbook, Complete Lifestyle Plan)

Instant Pot for Two Cookbook: Easy and Delicious Recipes (Slow Cooker for 2, Healthy Dishes)

Ketogenic Instant Pot Cookbook: Easy, Delicious Recipes for Weight Loss (Pressure Cooker Meals, Quick Healthy Eating, Meal Plan)

Ketogenic Diet Recipes in 20 Minutes or Less:: Beginner's Weight Loss Keto Cookbook Guide (Ketogenic Cookbook, Complete Lifestyle Plan)

Standalone

Instant Pot for Two Cookbook for Beginners: A Mother's Guide

CPSIA information can be obtained
at www.ICGtesting.com
Printed in the USA
LVHW061411240521
688335LV00025B/1423